LEASING

LEASING

Brian Coyle

CIB PUBLISHING

FINANCIAL
EDUCATION

CIB Publishing
c/o The Chartered Institute of Bankers
Emmanuel House
4-9 Burgate Lane
Canterbury
Kent
CT1 2XJ
United Kingdom

Telephone: 01227 762600

CIB Publishing publications are published by The Chartered Institute of Bankers, a non-profit making registered educational charity.

The Chartered Institute of Bankers believes that the sources of information upon which the book is based are reliable and has made every effort to ensure the complete accuracy of the text. However, neither CIB, the author nor any contributor can accept any legal responsibility whatsoever for consequences that may arise from errors or omissions or any opinion or advice given.

Typeset by The Foundry
Printed by WBC Book Manufacturers, Bridgend

ISBN 0-85297-462-0

Contents

1

Introduction

Leasing can be an important source of asset finance for businesses. This book explains what leasing is, who uses lease finance and why, and how lease agreements are reached, as well as the commercial and financial reporting aspects of leasing.

What is Leasing?

A lease is an agreement in which the owner of an item, for example a business asset or a piece of real estate, allows someone else to use it for a specified time, in return for a rental. The owner of the leased asset is the lessor and the user of the asset is the lessee.

The definition of a lease is not completely standardized because of differences in taxation, commercial law or other regulatory features, though in the case of the US and the UK the definitions are broadly similar. Countries also use different terminology.

To many lessees, a lease is simply a rental agreement. However, rental agreements (or plant hire agreements) are generally short term, i.e. two years or less whereas commercial leases typically cover a period of several years.

When a new item of equipment is leased, for example a piece of agricultural machinery

- the lessor pays for the equipment, but
- the lessee takes delivery direct from the manufacturer or supplier.

The manufacturer or supplier is paid by the lessor, who then receives a stream of rental payments from the lessee.

Length of equipment leases: Europe 1996

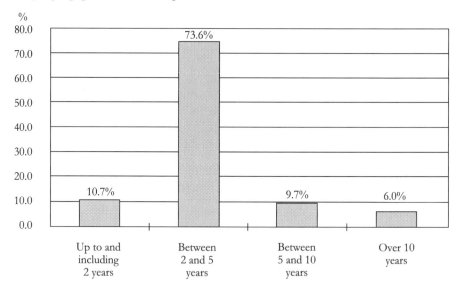

What Assets are Leased?

Commercial leasing has its origins in real estate leasing. Landowners, or owners of buildings, can lease their property to a tenant. The term leasing industry, however, usually refers to the leasing of business equipment or equipment leasing. The renting of domestic equipment to consumers,

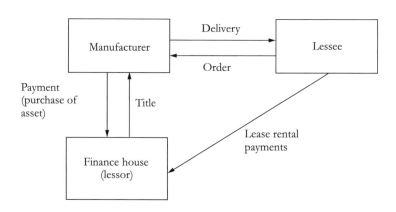

such as televisions and video recorders, falls outside the leasing industry.

Equipment Leasing

Trends and forecasts for equipment leasing in the US

Year	Business investment in equipment (Billions of dollars)	Equipment leasing volume (Billions of dollars)	Market penetration range (Percentage)
1988	348.4	112.7	32.3
1989	365.7	125.4	34.3
1990	388.3	124.3	32.0
1991	375.5	120.2	32.0
1992	376.2	121.7	32.3
1993	443.9	130.5	29.4
1994	487.0	140.2	28.8
1995	538.8	151.4	28.1
1996	566.2	169.9	30.0
1997	582.1	179.8	30.9
1998	593.0	183.4	30.9

Items of equipment that can be leased range from small items, such as cars, shop fittings, office furniture, printing machines, photocopiers and vending machines, to big ticket items such as ships, aircraft, satellites and entire industrial plants.

Any item of equipment that is in normal use with industry and commerce can be leased, with asset values ranging from several hundred dollars up to millions of dollars. The former is known as small-ticket leasing while lease financing over $2 million is known as big-ticket.

Leasing as a Source of Finance

For the lessee, equipment leasing is a source of medium-term finance. The purchase cost of the leased asset is financed by the lessor, and the rental payments by the lessee include both an interest charge as well as a capital repayment element.

Leasing is used by companies of all sizes and in all industries, as one method of financing their assets.

Volume by equipment type for 1997

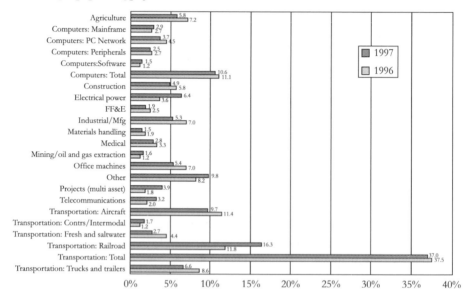

(*Source Equipment Leasing Association, updated August, 1998*)

Countries where leasing is used extensively include the US, Germany, the UK and France.

Sale and Leaseback

In a sale and leaseback agreement, the owner of an asset sells it to a finance company and then leases it back immediately, without ever surrendering the use of the asset. Sale and leaseback agreements provide the lessee with an immediate injection of cash into the business from the asset sale. With high value assets, such as land and buildings, the amount of financing can be substantial. Sale and leaseback can be arranged either

- immediately after purchase, or
- later during the asset's useful life, with the sale price reflecting its current value.

Novation

Sale and leaseback

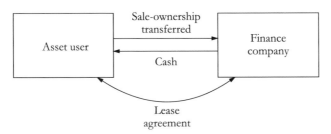

Novation involves a three-way agreement between the supplier of an asset, the user (lessee) and the lessor. The user places an order for the equipment with the supplier, and has certain rights and obligations under the purchase agreement.

The user then transfers certain rights and obligations to the lessor with the supplier's consent, e.g. title. The lessor then becomes the purchaser of the equipment leaving the lessee typically with the other benefits under the contract, e.g. warranties. Novation is common particularly in situations where there is a lengthy lead-time between ordering the equipment and delivery.

Who are the Lessors?

Most lease finance is provided by specialist leasing companies that can be

- the leasing subsidiary of a commercial bank or financial institution
- a captive finance subsidiary of a major manufacturer where the leasing activity is an aspect of the company's sales/marketing function

- an independent leasing company, whether small and specialized or large and diversified
- Others, such as investment bankers and independent brokers/packagers who bring the parties of a lease together.

In the US more than 700 equipment leasing and finance companies belong to the principal leasing body, the Equipment Leasing Association of America (ELA) that was founded in 1961. ELA members agree to follow the association's Code of Fair Business Practices that advocates confidentiality regarding the lessee's financial information as well as proper disclosure to the lessee of all relevant information regarding the terms and conditions of the lease.

A number of UK clearing banks have a finance house subsidiary to carry out much (or all) of their leasing business. Some banks use a finance house to provide lease finance for small and medium-ticket value transactions, but have a separate subsidiary for big-ticket items.

The US leasing market is largely dominated by non-bank financial organizations such as GE Capital, AT&T Capital and Xerox Corporation and by those with strong manufacturer links such as IBM Credit. But even though most non-bank financial organizations started out by leasing only equipment supplied by their parent company, nearly all now lease third-party equipment as well.

Despite the dominance of non-bank financial organizations in the US some bank-based companies still command a large market share. These include Citicorp, Newcourt Credit Group that acquired another bank-owned company, The CIT Group, in March 1999 in a $9 billion stock transaction, and Orix whose shareholders include several Japanese banks as well as State Street Bank and Trust Company.

In contrast, the UK leasing market is largely dominated by subsidiaries of the major clearing banks. A number of UK clearing banks have a finance house subsidiary to carry out much if not all of their leasing business. Some banks use a finance house to provide lease finance for small and medium-ticket value transactions, but have a separate subsidiary for big-ticket items.

A captive company is one that is owned and financed by a manufacturer, and specializes in leasing the manufacturer's products to customers. This is known as vendor leasing, or sometimes sales aid leasing in the UK. Whereas an independent leasing company is primarily concerned with making a profit by providing lease finance, captive companies share the same marketing objectives as the parent company. The manufacturer can decide the terms of the lease and offer leasing as part of its service to customers. Examples of captives are IBM Credit, Pitney Bowes Credit, and the financing arms of vehicle manufacturers.

Independent specialist leasing companies include multinationals, such as Comdisco Inc, Newcourt Credit Group and Capital Associates International. And although GE Capital is a wholly owned subsidiary of General Electric (GE), it also provides lease finance for a wide range of assets and to a wide range of industrial and commercial sectors. GE Capital is virtually an independent-leasing company despite its parent.

Many independents specialize in leasing particular types of equipment. For example, the Irish-based GPA Group leases commercial aircraft, Comdisco Inc leases and remarkets high-technology equipment and services and Genstar Container Corporation rents/leases marine and domestic cargo containers to shipping lines and railroads.

Most countries have national leasing associations that represent the best interests of members particularly regarding legislative matters. In the US the leading association is the Equipment Leasing Association (ELA). There are also regional associations as well as specialist associations for vehicles including the American Automotive Leasing Association (AALA), the National Vehicle Leasing Association (NVLA) and Truck Renting and Leasing Association (TRLA), and for computer resellers the Information Technology Resellers Association (ITRA). The leading UK association is the Finance and Leasing Association (FLA); in Germany, it is the Bundesverband Deutscher Leasing-Gesellschaften, and the body that represents 28 European leasing associations is the Brussels-based Leaseurope.

Ownership of Leased Assets

In a lease agreement, the legal owner of the asset is the lessor.

In most countries, a lease agreement can include terms for the eventual purchase of the asset by the lessee. The purchase option may be stated at a specified amount or at fair market value.

The finance lease (full-payout lease or capital lease) is one in which the lessor recovers, through the lease payments, all costs incurred in the lease plus an acceptable rate of return, without any reliance on the leased equipment's future residual value. It is generally a noncancelable agreement in which the lessee is responsible for maintenance, taxes and insurance. In the US a finance lease is often called a capital lease. This is explained in more detail in Chapter 4.

In the UK, a finance lease is defined more narrowly than in other countries. For tax reasons, there has to be a permanent separation of ownership and possession of the asset. The lessor retains ownership of the asset and the lessee does not have the option to buy it at any time, not even at the end of the lease period. If the hirer is able to buy the asset at the end of the hire period, the contract would be a hire purchase agreement in the UK, not a lease. And hire purchase agreements are treated differently from lease agreements under UK tax law.

Leasing and Conditional Sale Agreement

Both leasing and hire purchase are forms of asset finance used by companies to finance their acquisition of plant, machinery and equipment. In the US and the UK, the difference between them relates to

- the ownership of the asset, and
- entitlement to tax allowances.

Under a lease agreement the lessor owns the asset and can claim the tax allowances that are obtainable under tax law. However the lessee, the user of the asset, enjoys use of the equipment throughout the lease period, provided the rentals are paid and the conditions of the lease are observed.

Under a conditional sales lease (hire purchase in the UK) the user has conditional ownership of the asset, provided payments are made during the hire period. At the end of the hire period, a nominal fee is paid by the user to obtain full ownership. The tax allowances on the purchase cost are granted to the user because of the conditional ownership, and not to the provider of the finance.

In many countries a lease and a conditional sales agreement amount to the same thing because the lessee can buy the equipment outright at the end of the lease period.

Brief History of Leasing

Leasing has existed in some form for several thousand years. Records of leased land, agricultural equipment and oxen in the kingdoms of Sumeria have survived from about 3000BC.

Equipment leasing in its modern form developed during the Industrial Revolution, from the mid-18th century. During the 19th century in the UK, private investors financed the manufacture of coal wagons that were hired by coal owners to transport coal on the railways. The world's first regional leasing company, the Birmingham Wagon Company was established in 1855 to lease railway wagons to coal and mineral producers for periods of five to eight years. Leasing of railcars in the US evolved in the 1860s.

Tax regulations encouraged a rapid advance in leasing in the US from the 1950s and in the UK from the 1970s, resulting in the creation of lease finance companies to offer tax-based leases to businesses. Tax-based financial leasing occurs when leasing activity is encouraged by a favorable tax regime.

Conclusion

It should be stressed that leasing is just one of several sources of asset finance. It is useful to consider the various methods of acquiring assets that a company can choose.

The different types of lease, that include finance leases, operating leases and contract hire, and the reasons for choosing lease finance in preference to other methods of financing, are considered in the following chapters.

Methods of asset finance

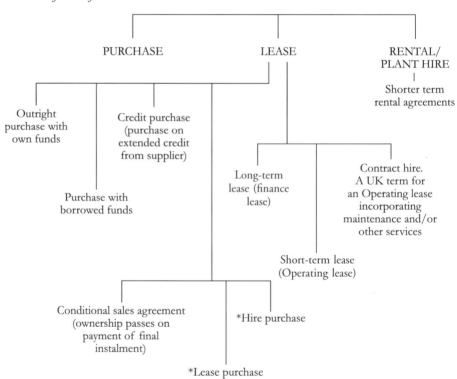

*Ownership passes for a nominal sum

2

Lease Structure

A lessor invests capital in purchasing an asset for leasing and expects to make a return on the investment. The return on investment consists of

- the rental payments, and
- in some cases, income from the eventual disposal of the asset at the end of the lease period.

The lease rentals and the lessor's income from the eventual disposal of the asset, taken together, should be sufficient for the lessor both to recover the capital cost of the asset and also to make a suitable return on the investment, allowing for the lessor's costs of finance and administration.

Finance Leases and Operating Leases

Leases can be divided into two broad categories. They are known as

- finance leases or full payout leases. The term capital lease is also synonymous with finance leases although the tax rules are more clearly defined, and
- operating leases also called true leases.

With a finance lease, the lessor expects to earn all, or almost all of his return on investment from the lease rentals. With an operating lease, the lessor relies to a fairly large extent for his investment return on the income from the eventual disposal of the asset at the end of the lease.

The terms and definitions for these two broad types of lease vary between different countries but the broad distinction between finance leases and operating leases is the same. These are described in further detail in chapters 3 and 4.

Terms of a Lease Agreement

A lease agreement between a lessor and a lessee relates to a specific asset or group of assets. The agreement should specify terms relating to

- choosing the asset ownership
- the lease period
- rental payments
- renewal options or asset disposal
- early termination
- equipment upgrades during the lease period.

Choosing the Asset

The lessee's choice of asset for leasing could be either unlimited or restricted to a specified range of models.

In many lease agreements, the lessee has complete freedom of choice in selecting the supplier and make of asset. For example, a company wishing to lease a heavy goods vehicle for its road transport fleet could be free to select the vehicle distributor and the make and model of vehicle. The lessor then provides the money to pay for the asset.

In some lease agreements, however, the user could be required to select from a specified range of models and from a particular supplier. This occurs when the lease finance is available to the lessee as part of the supplier's sales and marketing package. This is known as vendor finance or sales aid leasing.

Ownership

A finance lease, or a capital lease, is where the leased asset is owned by the lessor for the duration of the lease, but is in the possession of the lessee. At the end of the rental period, a finance lease provides for further rentals at a low rate whereas a conditional sales agreement, or hire purchase allows the lessee to purchase the asset at a bargain purchase rate. The differences are straightforward

- a finance lease leaves ownership with the lessor until the asset is eventually scrapped or sold to a third party at the end of the rental period. Capital allowances are claimed by the lessor
- a conditional sales agreement is where the user, i.e. the lessee, claims the capital allowances.

Lease Period

A lease allows the lessee use of the asset for a specified period. With a short-term finance lease, where the lessee has possession of the asset for most of its useful life, there is

- a primary period for the lease, and
- a secondary period.

During the primary period, the lessor will receive sufficient rental payments from the lessee to cover the cost of the asset, plus interest and profit.

At the end of the primary period, the lessee could decide to stop using the asset. The terms of the lease agreement should cover the arrangements for returning the asset to the lessor, or for disposing of the asset on behalf of the lessor with the lessee acting as the lessor's agent in the sale.

In many finance lease agreements, however, the lessee is given the option to continue leasing the asset on an annual basis after the end of the primary period. During this secondary lease period, only a nominal annual rental is charged, typically about 0.25% to 1% of the original cost of the asset.

Obsolescence Risk and Maintenance

During the primary period of a finance lease, the lessee bears the risk of obsolescence of the equipment. If the equipment becomes out-of-date, and superseded by a new and better product, the lessee must continue to use it, or pay a termination fee to cancel the lease. With many leased items, this risk is low. Occasionally, however, the pace of technological change, for example in computer equipment, can be rapid, and a lessee might therefore prefer a shorter-term operating lease to a longer-term finance lease. If the asset has become obsolete, the lessor will be unable to sell it at the hoped-for price. The former lessee, on the other hand, will be free to switch to using a more up-to-date product. With short-term leases most of the obsolescence risk falls on the lessor.

The responsibility for maintaining the equipment during the lease period could lie with either the lessor or the lessee. With finance leases, however, the lessee usually undertakes to maintain the asset in good working order.

Rental Payments

Rentals that are quoted to customers depend on several key factors

- the interest rate charged on the finance
- the length of the primary lease period
- the expected residual value of the leased asset at the end of the primary period
- the credit rating of the lessee
- the capital value of the lease, i.e. the size of the lease financing
- the extent to which the leasing company wants the leasing deal. This is a condition of competition in the leasing market. A leasing company could quote lower rentals, reducing the profit element, in order to win the business.

The rental payments in the primary period of a lease should allow the lessor to

- recover all (or nearly all) the cost of the asset

- cover administrative expenses and bad debts
- cover the lessor's interest costs
- provide the lessor with a profit.

The interest rate element in the lease rental should give the leasing company a profit margin over the cost of its own funds and administration costs. For example, if a leasing company can raise funds at 8% per annum, the finance charge in the lease rentals must be at an effective interest rate of over 8% to yield a profit for the lessor.

The interest rate charged to the borrower can vary according to the quantity and value of assets leased to the customer and the customer's credit rating.

The residual value that the leasing company puts on the asset at the end of the lease can affect the lease rental significantly, particularly for short-term (operating) leases.

Example
A leasing company is arranging a two-year lease for a car costing $10,000. Its estimated residual value after two years is $6,000. The lessee will pay rentals monthly in advance, and the interest rate charged by the lessor will be 8% per annum (0.67% per month).

Analysis
The lease rentals must be sufficient to cover the fall in the value of the asset over the two-year period from $10,000 to $6,000. However, if the estimated residual value after two years is only $5,000, the rental payments would have to be higher to cover the bigger fall in value. Profits are therefore very much dependent on the market for second-hand cars at the end of the rental period.

Allowing for the monthly payments in advance and the interest rate of 8%, the monthly rentals charged by the lessor would be as follows. Workings are not shown.

Residual value	Rental		Total rentals over 2 years
$	$		$
6,000	219.45	(x 24)	5,266.80
5,000	257.75	(x 24)	6,168.00

The residual value of leased assets varies according to the age of the assets. Putting an estimate on residual values for different types, makes and ages of asset calls for very careful judgment, even when there is a liquid secondhand market in the asset, e.g. autombiles.

For credit-risk reasons, lessors usually prefer rental payments in advance rather than in arrears. Payments are commonly at quarterly intervals. Some leases, particularly small units, often require payments monthly in advance to act as an early warning signal for potential problems. Six-monthly or annual rentals also occur, particularly for big-ticket items.

The rental payments for many leases are fixed equal amounts. The lessor is therefore providing fixed interest finance over the entire lease period. Over the primary period of a finance lease, rentals comprise a capital repayment element and an interest element. The early payments consist more of interest charges and less of capital repayment, whereas the later payments consist more of capital repayments.

A lessor's rate of recovery of the capital cost involved is illustrated in the following example.

Example
A leasing company leases equipment to a lessee for a four-year period. Rentals are payable six-monthly in advance, and the interest charge to the lessee is 5% each six months, i.e. 10% per annum semi-annual that is 10.25% per annum compound.

The equipment costs $339,319 and will have no residual value at the end of four years.

Analysis

The six-monthly rental, payable in advance, will be $50,000. The workings are not shown, but are illustrated in the table below.

Half-year	Opening capital balance	Rental in advance	Net capital balance before interest	Interest at 5% per half year	Closing capital balance
	$	$	$	$	$
0 (start)	339,319	50,000	289,319	14,466	303,785
1	303,785	50,000	253,785	12,689	266,474
2	266,474	50,000	216,474	10,824	227,298
3	227,298	50,000	177,298	8,865	186,163
4	186,163	50,000	136,163	6,808	142,971
5	142,971	50,000	92,971	4,649	97,620
6	97,620	50,000	47,620	2,380	50,000
7	50,000	50,000	0	-	-

The eight rental payments of $50,000 consist of capital repayments and interest charges as follows:

Half-year	Total rental	Interest element	Capital element
	$	$	$
0	50,000	14,466	35,534
1	50,000	12,689	37,311
2	50,000	10,824	39,176
3	50,000	8,865	41,135
4	50,000	6,808	43,192
5	50,000	4,649	45,351
6	50,000	2,380	47,620
7	50,000	0	50,000
	400,000	60,681	339,319

The recovery of capital cost (with a fixed interest profile) can be shown in a graph, as follows:

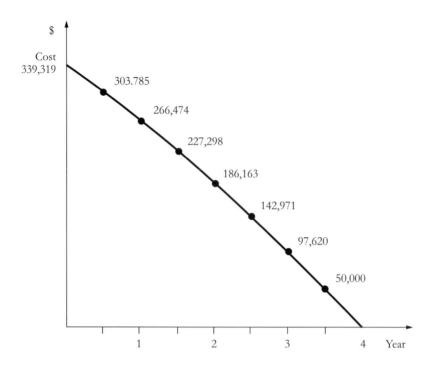

Quoting Rental Prices

Rentals are usually quoted at a rate per $1,000 (or $1,000, etc.) of equipment cost; for example $115 per $1,000 payable quarterly in advance for five years. In the example above, the rental is $147.35 per $1,000 of cost ($50,000 ÷ $339,319 x $1,000) payable in advance every six months for four years.

Occasionally, a nominal rate of interest may be quoted. In the example above, the interest rate is 5% every six months. This would be quoted as 10% per annum, payable every six months. The effective rate of interest (annual percentage rate or APR) based on the number of compounding periods per annum, for six-monthly payments of 5%, is 10.25%, but the nominal rate of 10% is quoted.

With some leasing, particularly for small-ticket, fairly low-cost items, salespeople could be given a rate card, quoting lease rentals as a rate per thousand for a particular type of asset such as automobiles or photocopiers, for different lease periods and different frequencies of rental payment, for example monthly or quarterly.

Tailored Rentals

In some long-term lease agreements, rental payments can be structured to meet the special requirements of the lessee, by taking into consideration the lessee's anticipated operating cash flows from using the leased assets. The most common tailored rental patterns, seasonal, stepped, deferred and ballooned payments, are described in Chapter 4.

Rental Variation Clauses

Some lease agreements contain one or more rental variation clauses, so that the amount of each rental payment is not fixed over the primary lease period. Rental variations in finance leases could be triggered by various events, such as a change in interest rates, a change in the rate of corporation tax or the non-receipt of a government grant. Operating leases could include an index-linking clause, whereby periodic rentals are increased in line with the rise in a suitable cost index. Rental variation clauses are described more fully in Chapter 4.

Lessor's Administrative Costs

A lessor will expect the rental payments to cover all out-of-pocket expenses and administrative costs. These can be high, particularly for big-ticket items during the period when the lease is being negotiated. Costs will include legal fees, fees for accountancy services, and survey and valuation fees. The lessor can arrange to cover expenses and administrative costs

- by quoting rentals that include a specific charge to cover the lessor's costs, any under- or over-estimate will be a direct cost or profit to the lessor
- by capitalizing the expenses, so that the rental payments are set at a level whereby the expenses will be recovered with interest over the primary lease period
- by means of a separate payment by the lessee that will cover specific expenses.

Cost per Copy Agreements

In the case of photocopier leasing, rental payments can be agreed as a cost per copy. The lessee pays a fixed amount for each copy produced by the machine. The payment by the lessee covers the lessor's finance cost (capital recovery and interest) and service.

Renewal Options or Asset Disposal

At the end of the lease period, the asset could be

- returned to the lessor for renting to another user
- sold
- purchased by the lessee
- rented or leased by the lessee for a further period.

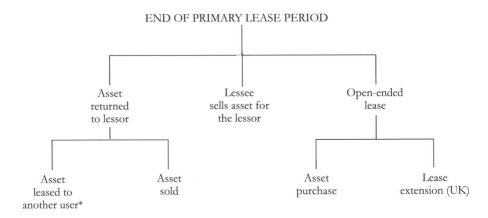

* This option is more likely to occur with short-term operating leases for assets with a liquid secondhand market, such as vehicles, or computers or perhaps printing machines or aircraft.

Renewal Options: Secondary Lease Periods

In most finance (capital) lease agreements, excluding UK finance leases, the lessee has an option or gives an undertaking to purchase the asset at the end of the lease period. In the US and UK, most finance leases include an option for the lessee to continue to use the asset after the primary period by extending the lease for a secondary period, at a much lower rental than in the primary lease period. During the primary period the lessor expects to recover the full capital cost of the asset, its money and its profit. The amount of the rental in the secondary period is fixed by the original lease agreement.

The secondary period can be

- for a fixed number of years
- arranged on a year-by-year basis, with an option to terminate every year
- for an indefinite period, with the lessee able to terminate the agreement at any time subject to a minimum notice period.

With some leases for high-value assets (big-ticket leases), there could be several renewal periods. At the end of the primary lease period there could be a secondary lease period with a fixed duration. At the end of this period there could be a further option to extend the lease into a tertiary period at an even lower rental.

In some lease contracts, the lessee could be required to give notice of termination before the end of the primary lease period. Unless notice is given, the lessee must continue to rent the equipment for a further period, of perhaps one year. A lease contract could also give the lessor the right to take possession of the asset at the end of the lease period, by giving notice to the lessee before the period ends.

Asset Disposal

When the lessee does not wish to continue using the asset at the end of the primary lease period, the asset could be returned to the lessor, to be rented out to another user, sold or scrapped. Leasing companies will often prefer to avoid the administrative burden of asset disposal. A lease agreement could therefore allow the lessee to act as an agent for the lessor in selling the asset to a third party buyer. The lessor thereby avoids the administrative difficulty of having to take physical possession of the asset before reselling it. In the US, an open-end lease is a conditional sale agreement in which the lessee guarantees that the lessor will realize a minimum value from the sale of the asset at the end of the lease.

The lessor of a long-term (finance) lease should have recovered most or all of the capital cost of the asset from rentals received over the primary lease period. In such cases where the lessee sells the asset on the lessor's behalf, it is usual for the lessor to pass on most of the sale proceeds to the lessee. Normally about 95% of the sale proceeds are passed on to the lessee, typically as a rebate on lease rentals. This method of disposal preserves the lessor's tax benefits for entering into the original lease.

The sale of the asset to the lessee at the end of the primary lease period is common in many countries. For example, in the US the lessee can buy the equipment at its residual value, and some lease agreements specify what the residual value will be, thereby fixing the sale price in advance. An open-ended lease is a conditional sale lease in which the lessee guarantees that the lesor will realize a minimum value from the sale of the asset at the end of the lease.

Early Termination

The primary period of a lease is usually non-cancelable by either the lessor or the lessee, although the lessor can take action in the event of default by the lessee and non-payment of rentals. The lessor, however, usually will be prepared to allow the lessee to terminate the lease during the primary period in return for a sufficient payment in compensation.

The most common method for calculating the amount of an early termination payment is to assess the value to the lessor of the remaining rental payments due up to the end of the primary lease period. The future rentals are discounted to a present value that is the amount of the termination payment.

Example

A lessee wishes to terminate a lease before the end of the primary period by making a termination payment. The termination payment would be made on the date that the next rental is due. There are eight quarterly rental payments

Analysis

The termination payment is the present value of future rental payments, discounted at an interest rate of 1% per quarter. The termination payment coincides with the date of the next rental, and the termination payment therefore is calculated as follows

Payment	Amount	Discount factor (1% per quarter)	Present value
	$		$
1	15,000	1.0	15,000
2	15,000	$\dfrac{1}{(1.01)^1}$	14,857
3	15,000	$\dfrac{1}{(1.01)^2}$	14,704
4	15,000	$\dfrac{1}{(1.01)^3}$	14,559
5	15,000	$\dfrac{1}{(1.01)^4}$	14,415
6	15,000	$\dfrac{1}{(1.01)^5}$	14,272
7	15,000	$\dfrac{1}{(1.01)^6}$	14,131
8	15,000	$\dfrac{1}{(1.01)^7}$	13,991
		Termination payment	115,923

Walkaway Options

A finance lease could offer the lessee an opportunity to terminate the lease in the middle of the primary period, without significant penalty. The lessee can walk away from the lease and return the asset to the lessor. The effect of a walkaway option is to give a finance lease characteristics similar to an operating lease.

A walkaway option could be exercisable by the lessee only on condition that the lessee takes on a new finance lease, perhaps with an upgraded item of equipment.

Advantages of Leasing

The advantages of leasing will be assessed more fully in later chapters. It is useful from the outset, however, to have a broad understanding of the potential benefits for both lessee and lessor.

Benefits for the Lessee

The features of equipment lease finance that could be attractive to lessees are summarized briefly in the following chart.

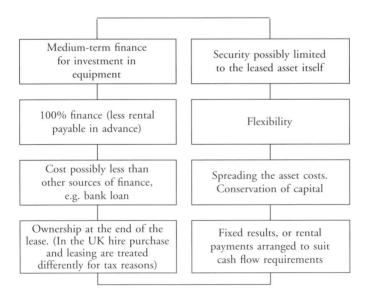

Medium-term finance for investment in equipment	Security possibly limited to the leased asset itself
100% finance (less rental payable in advance)	Flexibility
Cost possibly less than other sources of finance, e.g. bank loan	Spreading the asset costs. Conservation of capital
Ownership at the end of the lease. (In the UK hire purchase and leasing are treated differently for tax reasons)	Fixed results, or rental payments arranged to suit cash flow requirements

100% Medium-Term Finance

For the lessee, leasing is primarily a source of finance to fund the acquisition of business assets. A finance lease provides medium-term asset finance and can be an alternative to a bank loan. In many cases, lease finance can be obtained for a longer term than a bank would be willing to lend. There could even be occasions when lease finance is available whereas bank lending is not.

Unlike some forms of bank lending, e.g. a borrowing facility, a lease is for a minimum initial period and cannot be withdrawn by the lessor before the end of the period. Since the lessor buys the asset from the supplier, the lessee receives finance for the full cost of the asset. However, since it is usual for lease agreements to provide for rentals in advance, the lessor in effect finances the purchase cost minus the first rental payment.

A lease can also preserve the lessee's capacity to borrow. The lessor's only security for the debt could be the leased asset itself, whereas with a loan, the lending bank could ask for greater security, for example. a fixed charge on the purchased asset plus a floating charge over other assets of the business.

Cost

A major benefit of leasing can be competitive pricing of the lease finance, compared to other sources of finance. Since rentals are usually fixed in advance, finance leases provide the lessee with a fixed cost of finance over a period of several years. This gives the lessee protection against the effect of any subsequent rise in interest rates. In contrast, when an asset is purchased with a floating rate bank loan, the lessee is exposed to the risk of an increase in market rates of interest. Fixed rate asset financing can be particularly beneficial when the lessee wishes to hedge against the risk of rising interest rates and finance costs.

Leasing assets can also be more tax-efficient than buying them, depending on the tax position of the lessee, the normal life of the asset and the planned period of the lease. (Tax aspects are the subject of Chapter 8.) Leasing companies can raise funds more cheaply than most other companies and can also obtain the tax benefits of purchasing the assets for leasing. They can therefore offer leases to customers at a rate of interest that compares favorably with bank loans.

Ownership
When the lessee is able to obtain ownership of the asset at the end of the primary lease period, this can be an advantage provided that the asset's useful life is longer than the primary lease period.

Security for the Lessor
In a lease agreement, the lessor's security against non-payment by the lessee could be restricted to a fixed charge over the leased asset. The lessee would not have to give extra security, such as a floating charge over stocks and debtors.

However, there has been a noticeable change in the attitude of lessors in recent years, partly due to the high level of bad debts during the early 1990s, and partly due to the fall in the second-hand values of many assets. In the late 1980s, for example, a lessor could expect the second-hand value of a top quality printing machine such as a Heidelberg to be about 70% of cost after five years. The printing machine itself therefore would have provided adequate security for the lessor. This situation no longer applies because the secondhand value of printing machines is now much lower.

Most leasing companies have adopted the view that it is not sufficient to lend against the asset itself as collateral, and ask for more security. As a result there has been a move away from true asset finance that leasing used to represent.

Conserve Cash and Spread Costs
Provided the lessee makes the lease rental payments on schedule, the lessor cannot demand accelerated payments during the initial primary lease period when the payment schedule is fixed by agreement. The rental payments therefore spread the cost of using the asset over the primary lease

period in a cash flow pattern that is determined by the lease agreement.

Leases can also give the lessee flexibility, by negotiating rental payments to match the anticipated cash flows from using the leased asset. Rental payments spread the cost of the asset over a period of time, during which cash can be earned by using the asset to meet the rental payments. A road haulage company, for example, can spread the cost of new vehicles over a three- or four-year period in a leasing arrangement, and use the haulage income from the vehicles to pay their rental costs.

The pattern of rental payments can be adjusted in the lease negotiations, to allow for any build up in cash flows over the life of the asset. This can be done by means of a stepped lease or deferred payment lease or by allowing for seasonal variations in the lessee's annual cash flows.

One of the major advantages of leasing for the lessee is the ability to conserve capital. Publicity material of one US leasing corporation, states: "Because of the sizeable cash outlay involved in purchasing new equipment, many businesses lease to conserve capital. Money that could be used to buy inventory, advertise, hire personnel, is better spent doing just that rather than spent purchasing equipment that is worth less and less as time goes by. If you are in a business where you have important alternative uses for money on hand, leasing always wins out in the lease versus buy analysis."

Flexibility
Many leases are negotiated on terms that are tailored to the lessee's individual needs. The lessee usually can select the equipment and supplier. In addition, the pattern of rental payments can be adjusted, if required, to suit the lessee's operational cash flow by means of deferred payments, seasonally-adjusted payments, stepped leases or balloon payments.

The lessee also has a certain amount of flexibility in the period for which the asset is used. The lease can be extended at the end of the primary period or, at a cost, can be terminated early with the lessor's agreement. Some operating leases allow the lessee to upgrade or replace the asset before the end of the primary lease period, by taking on a new lease for new and upgraded items of equipment.

Convenience

The lessor should try to make leasing a convenient method of finance for creditworthy customers, because writing leases is the source of the lessor's profits. Leasing companies recognize that complex documentation and procedures for negotiating a lease can deter potential lessees. Documentation for leases and procedures for processing lease applications have therefore been simplified with the exception of leases for more expensive items.

For example, a company or local government authority can arrange a line of credit with a leasing company. The leasing company agrees to finance asset purchases up to the credit limit. Within this limit, the lessee can make its own asset purchase decisions, knowing that the credit will be readily available.

Off Balance-Sheet Finance

Another advantage sometimes claimed for leasing relates to financial reporting requirements. (These are explained in detail in Chapter 11.) There are two ways in which a company that uses leased assets, i.e. the lessee, can account for the assets in its balance sheet. It can either

- exclude the assets entirely from its balance sheet, keep them off-balance sheet on the grounds that they belong to the lessor, or
- show the leased assets as fixed assets in the balance sheet and also show a financial liability to the lessor, on the grounds that they are, for all practical purposes, the property of the lessee, who has unrestricted use of them.

The accounting rules about whether leased assets should be reported on the lessee's balance sheet, or whether they should be kept off balance sheet, vary between countries and according to whether the type of lease is finance lease or operating lease.

28

In the US and UK for example, items obtained under finance lease agreements must be shown in the lessee's accounts as a fixed asset with a capital liability to the lessor shown as a debt. However no such requirement applies to assets held under operating lease agreements. Usually these are shown only in the notes to the accounts. A company therefore can keep a substantial amount of its operating assets off the balance sheet by entering into operating leases. The effect of keeping lease finance off the balance sheet is to reduce the reported debt obligations of the lessee, and so reduce the amount of leverage.

On occasions, this can disguise the financial position of the company. In November 1993 for example, it was revealed that the troubled UK hotels group, Queens Moat Houses, had sold some of its German hotels to directors and senior managers and leased them back. These transactions removed DM270 million of debt off the group's balance sheet, and under the group's accounting policies applying at the time, could have added up to $32 million to the group's reported operating profit for the year in which the transactions occurred. This shows the need to understand the accounting standards and conventions used to draw up annual accounts.

Benefits and Risks for Lessors

Leasing companies benefit primarily from the profits made on their leasing activities.

A bank could benefit commercially from having a leasing subsidiary that would offer a full range of financial/lending services to customers, thus enhancing the bank's relationship with its business customers. The tax benefits for the lessor could make leasing more profitable than lending.

Leasing also can be used by a manufacturer as a sales aid, and contributes towards achieving higher sales turnover and profits and also greater control over the secondhand market for its products. A manufacturer could set up a finance subsidiary with sufficient funds to provide lease finance to customers, as in the case of Pitney Bowes Finance. More commonly, however, a manufacturer arranges sales and leasing through an external finance company.

A lessor must accept various risks in providing lease finance. There is a credit risk that the lessee will fail to make rental payments, or will be a late payer. A credit appraisal is carried out on prospective lessees, and a leasing company can refuse a lease or set an overall limit on a lessee's credit.

In the event of default by the lessee, the lessor can seek repayment through a claim on the secured asset or assets of the lessee. There is of course a risk that the value of the secured asset in a forced sale could be less than the capital repayment outstanding and still to be recovered.

The risk from an unexpected drop in asset residual values, perhaps due to obsolescence, is greatest however with operating leases. With these leases, the lessor depends to a significant extent on income from the disposal of the asset to achieve a target return on investment.

For leases without variation clauses, the lessor fixes the rental payments on the basis of assumptions about what the rates of corporation tax and interest will be. If tax rates or interest rates move adversely, a leasing company could find its profit margins squeezed by rising costs but fixed rental income.

As owner of the equipment, in some circumstances a lessor could be liable for claims by third parties for losses arising out of the use of the asset. A lessor usually will be indemnified against such claims by the lessee, and also could be entitled to the proceeds from insurance claims for insurance covering the equipment against third party liabilities.

3

Operating Leases

In an operating lease, the primary rental period is much shorter than the asset's expected useful life. At the end of the lease period, the asset will have a significant residual value. The lessor could sell the asset in the secondhand market, and the lessor's total returns from the asset will be

● the lease rentals, plus
● the sale value of the asset at the end of the lease period.

The lessor does not expect to recover the full capital of the asset from the lease rentals. In the US, an operating lease is defined as any lease that is not a capital lease. (See Chapter 4). The lessee can acquire the use of equipment for a fraction of the useful life of the asset. Additional services such as maintenance and insurance may be provided by the lessor.

In the UK an operating lease is usually determined by ensuring that the present value of the minimum lease payments is less than 90% of the fair value of the leased asset. This ensures that the lessor retains a significant economic interest in the residual value of the asset and is the most important difference between an operating lease and a full payout (finance) lease.

Features of Operating Leases

Operating leases are commonly regarded by lessees as rental agreements. An operating lease is typically for two or three years, but could be longer. Because they have a shorter duration than finance leases for similar types of asset, the terms operating lease and short-term lease can mean the same.

In an operating lease, the lessee does not have any interest in long-term ownership or long-term use of the asset. The lessor expects to gain possession of the asset at the end of the rental period. The lessee will not be expected to sell the asset on behalf of the lessor, and will not receive any share of the sale proceeds.

An operating lease can be attractive to users who do not want the asset for its full useful life, possibly because they have a policy of continually modernizing or upgrading their assets, e.g. IT managers wanting a technology refresh every two to three years. Operating leases are only attractive to a lessor when there is a reasonably liquid secondhand market in the assets. There has been widespread use of operating leases for marketable assets such as motor vehicles, computers, aircraft and printing machines.

Example
A TV production company wishes to obtain post-production editing equipment costing $200,000 under a two-year lease agreement. The leasing company estimates that the asset has an expected economic life of five years, and at the end of the second year would have a resale value of $80,000.

Lease rentals would be payable quarterly in advance. The leasing company will require a return on investment of 10.38% per annum compound that represents a return of 2.5% per quarter. In this example, taxation is ignored to simplify the illustration.

Analysis
The lessor can set the operating lease rental payments at an amount that will give a 10.38% per annum return on investment, taking into account the estimated sale value of the asset after two years.

Ignoring the effects of taxation, a rental of $18,279 per quarter would give this return, as illustrated in the table overleaf. The table shows the present value of the lease rentals discounted at 2.5% per quarter and the present value of the asset's residual value after two years, discounted at the same rate (10.38% per annum). Their combined present value is the amount of the lessor's current investment, $200,000.

Time period	Item	Amount	Discount factor at 2.5% per quarter	Present value
		$		$
0	1st rental	18,279	1.0	18,279
1	2nd rental	18,279	$\frac{1}{(1.025)^1}$	17,833
2	3rd rental	18,279	$\frac{1}{(1.025)^2}$	17,398
3	4th rental	18,279	$\frac{1}{(1.025)^3}$	16,974
4	5th rental	18,279	$\frac{1}{(1.025)^4}$	16,560
5	6th rental	18,279	$\frac{1}{(1.025)^5}$	16,156
6	7th rental	18,279	$\frac{1}{(1.025)^6}$	15,762
7	8th rental	18,279	$\frac{1}{(1.025)^7}$	15,377
				134,339
End of Year 2 Residual value		80,000	$\frac{1}{(1.025)^8}$	65,661
	Total present value of returns			200,000

The lessor is relying on the estimated value of the asset after two years to provide the required return on investment. If the asset's value exceeds $80,000 after two years, the lessor will achieve a return in excess of target, but if the residual value is below $80,000, the lessor's investment return will fall below the target.

A lessor does not have to sell an asset at the end of an operating lease. The same equipment can be leased to a different lessee, in a new lease agreement. In some cases such as airplanes, the same asset can be leased several times to different lessees, during its useful life.

Maintenance and Insurance

It is very important to the lessor that the leased asset should be in good condition at the end of an operating lease, otherwise the asset cannot be sold at its estimated residual value or leased to a different user. The documentation normally will require the lessee to return the equipment on time, to a specific location and in good working order and condition. For example automobile leases obligate the hirer to pay for any dents or damage that would depress the vehicle's secondhand value. Insurance and maintenance are generally more significant to the lessor with operating leases than with finance leases.

4

Finance Leases

In a finance lease, also called a full payout lease, a financing lease or a capital lease, the lessor relies almost entirely on the lease rentals to recover the cost of his investment in the asset. The residual value of the asset is of little or no significance to the lessor.

Features of a Finance Lease

The length of the primary lease period usually covers most of the expected useful life of the asset. A primary lease period covering more than 75% of the asset's useful life would be typical, although there is wide variation. Three- to five-year primary lease periods are common, five years is typical for plant and machinery items, and periods of about 10 years are usual for ships, airplane and railway rolling stock.

It is essential that the lease rentals in the primary lease period must be sufficient for the lessor

- to recover the full cost of the asset
- to cover his own financing cost
- to cover administrative expenses and bad debts
- to earn a profit.

The lessee is required to insure and maintain the asset. Because the lessee will use the asset for most of, or even all of its life, if the asset is leased for a secondary period after the end of the primary period, and is responsible for its insurance and upkeep, most of the risks and rewards associated with ownership of the asset are transferred to the lessee. But for tax reasons, legal ownership, remains with the lessor.

Recovery of Capital Investment and Residual Values

When the lessor intends to dispose of the asset at the end of the primary lease period, the lessee could agree if it is in the lease contract, to act as the lessor's selling agent. In return, the lessee could receive as much as 95% of the sales proceeds as a rebate on rentals.

Example
In a four-year lease agreement, a lessee acquires an asset costing $55,000. Rental payments are $4,000 quarterly, in advance. The agreement provides for the lessee to sell the asset after four years on behalf of the lessor, and to receive a rental rebate equal to 90% of the net sales proceeds. The net sales proceeds after four years were $20,000.

Analysis
Although the residual value of the asset is $20,000, 90% of this ($18,000) will be paid to the lessee, leaving only $2,000 for the lessor. The lessor makes most of his return on investment from the 16 lease rental payments of $4,000 each.

Under recovery of Capital Cost

With some finance leases, however, the lessor places a residual value on the asset at the end of this period, and is therefore willing to charge a rental that does not recover the capital cost in full in the primary lease period. This situation can arise if

- the lease provides for a period of compulsory extension at the end of the primary period
- the lessor has an option to sell the equipment to a third party, perhaps a supplier or distributor, at a pre-arranged price at the end of the primary lease period.

Where a lease provides for a compulsory extension at the end of the primary period, the lessee is obliged to continue to pay rentals, although a lower amount than during the primary period, during a secondary lease period, for a minimum length of time. The lessor therefore will be able to recover some of the capital value of the asset during the extension period, and does not have to recover 100% of the capital value during the primary period.

If the lessor has an option to sell the asset to a third party at the end of the primary lease period, the lessor (and not the lessee) will receive the residual value when the asset is sold to the third party. Because the lessor does not need to recover the full capital value of the asset from the lease rentals and the sale price is fixed in advance, it can afford to charge a lower rental without any risk that the residual value of the asset will fall.

Example

A captive leasing company provides lease finance to a client for the acquisition of telecommunications equipment. It includes an arrangement whereby the equipment can be sold back to the internal sales company at 10% of original cost. The equipment costs $20,000 and this structure allows the leasing company or manufacturer to reduce the periodic rentals and retain control of the equipment on expiry.

The lessee will pay rentals quarterly in advance for the three years.

The leasing company requires a return of 3% per quarter (a nominal return of 12% per annum). Taxation will be ignored for the purpose of this illustration.

Analysis

If the leasing company did not have the arrangement to sell the equipment after three years, or if the leasing company allowed the lessee to sell the assets as an agent and receive the sale income, the full capital cost of the equipment would have to be recovered from the lease rentals. Each rental would be $1,951.

However, since the leasing company will receive 10% of the original cost (in this example, $2,000) from selling it after three years, the lease rentals can be reduced to $1,813 per quarter.

The present value of rentals of $1,813 per quarter (payable in advance) for three years, discounted at 3% per quarter, is $18,597. This means that 93% of the capital value of $20,000 would be recovered by the lessor from the primary lease rentals. The remaining portion of the capital value would be recovered from selling the assets for $2,000 at the end of the third year.

Summary

Recovery of capital during primary period	Lease rental (quarterly in advance)
%	$
100	1,951
93	1,813

Definitions of a Finance Lease

Different countries have defined finance leases in slightly different ways. In the US, Financial Accounting Standards Board (FASB) 13, for example defines a capital lease as one where the lease contract provides for any one of the following

- ownership of the asset to be transferred eventually to the lessee
- a bargain purchase option for the lessee at the end of the primary lease period
- a primary lease term of 75% or more of the asset's expected economic life
- the present value of the minimum lease rental payments (discounted at the lessor's cost of capital) exceeds 90% of the fair market value of the asset less related investment tax credits retained by the lessor.

Any lease that is not a capital lease is defined as an operating lease.

Within the UK a formal definition of a finance lease is provided by the

Statement of Standard Accounting Practice 21 "Accounting for Leases and Hire Purchase Contracts" (1984).

A finance lease is defined in SSAP21 as "a lease that transfers substantially all the risks and rewards of ownership of an asset to the lessee". It should be presumed that substantially all the risks and rewards of ownership have been transferred to the lessee if the lessor expects to recover all or most of the "fair value" of the asset from rental payments in the minimum (i.e. primary) lease period. In other words, if the lessor expects to recover all (or nearly all) of the capital value of the asset from the single lease agreement, the lease should be considered a finance lease rather than an operating lease. An operating lease is defined by SSAP21 simply as a lease that is not a finance lease.

To determine whether most of the value of the asset will be recovered from the lease, the rental payments over the primary lease period should be discounted to a present value, using the interest rate implicit in the lease as the discount rate. If the present value of the lease payments is substantially all (90% or more) of the fair value of the asset, it should be presumed that the lease is a finance lease.

Example
A leasing company has entered into a five-year lease with a company for the use of scientific equipment costing $250,000. Rentals are $15,500 per quarter, payable in advance. The leasing company's interest rate is 2.4% per quarter equivalent to a nominal rate of 9.6% per annum, and an effective rate of 9.95% per annum.

The present value of $1 per quarter, payable in advance every quarter for five years, is $16.115 when discounted at a quarterly return of 2.4%.

Analysis
The present value of the rental payments over the primary lease period is as follows:

Rental		Discount factor		Present value
$15,500	x	16.115	=	$249,782.50

This is 99.9% of the cost of the asset. Assuming this to be the asset's fair value, the lease would be regarded as a finance (full pay-out or capital) lease, rather than an operating lease.

Operating and Finance Leases Compared

The differences between operating and finance leases are mainly differences of degree, and in many respects they are similar. The key difference, as described previously, is the treatment of the asset's residual value

- with an operating lease, the rental payments take account of the asset's expected residual value at the end of the lease period. The lessor takes the risk that the residual value could be lower
- in the case of a capital lease, the residual value of the asset is largely ignored in the rental payments. The lessee therefore takes the residual value risk.

The table overleaf provides a comparison of finance leases and operating leases.

Tailored Rental Payments

Rental payments on finance leases can be structured to meet the specific requirements of the lessee. The lessee could want the rental payments on the asset to be matched by cash flows that are earned from using the asset. These cash flows could be seasonal during the course of each year, or could build up over time as the project using the asset develops.

The most common types of tailored rental patterns are

- seasonal rentals
- stepped rentals
- deferred rentals, and
- balloon (or ballooned) rentals.

Finance Leases and Operating Leases Compared

	Finance lease	Operating lease	Lease purchase
Alternative terms	Capital lease (US), Lease rental	True lease (US), Operating rental, Rental	HP, Lease with option to purchase, Purchase lease (US), Dollar option lease (US)
Choice of asset	By the lessee	By the lessee, or available from the lessor's own equipment range	By the lessee
Primary lease period	Most of the asset's useful life, but not longer	Shorter than a finance lease for a similar asset	Most of the asset's useful life, but not longer
Secondary lease period	Lease period can often be extended, for a nominal rental	If the lease is extended, the rental will be at a market cost (based on the asset's current value)	Lessee purchases asset on expiry for nominal sum
Lease rentals	Sufficient to recover the capital cost of the asset. Total rentals payable higher than for operating lease	Usually the lessee's rentals alone are insufficient to provide the lessor's required return on investment. The residual value of the asset is significant	Sufficient to recover the capital cost of the asset. Total rentals payable higher than for a finance and operating lease
Residual value	Rentals cover the cost of the asset	Rental structure takes into account the estimated residual value of the asset to the lessor	Rentals cover the cost of the asset
Early termination	Early termination clause during the primary lease period is uncommon	Early termination sometimes allowed	Early termination clause during the primary period is uncommon
Maintenance and insurance	Lessee's responsibility	Lessee's responsibility. Lessor could impose more exacting requirements in the lease	Lessee's responsibility
Ownership (UK)	Asset owned at all times by the lessor during the lease period	Asset owned at all times by the lessor during the lease period	Asset owned by the lessor during rental period
Ownership (US and other countries outside the UK)	Lessee can purchase the asset at the end of the lease without affecting the tax position of the lessor or lessee. The purchase price is well below realizable value	Asset returned to lessor for sale or re-leasing	As Finance lease
Disposal at end of lease	In the US and UK, the lessee often acts as the lessor's agent to sell the asset. The lessee receives most of the sale proceeds	Asset returned to lessor for sale or re-leasing	Lessee purchases the asset for a nominal sum

41

Seasonal Rentals

Some companies have seasonal business cycles. Airline tour operators (leasing aircraft) can carry a higher volume of passengers in summer than in winter. Similarly, hotels (leasing catering equipment) could have their peak business at a particular time of the year depending on their location.

The rentals for leased equipment can be adjusted to the seasonal cash flow patterns of the lessee, with a higher rental in the peak business seasons and a lower rental in the quiet seasons.

Example

A hotel wishes to lease equipment costing $150,000 under a five-year full payout lease arrangement. Rentals would be payable six-monthly in advance, starting during the summer season. The hotel's business is seasonal, and it earns twice as much money in summer than in winter. It would therefore like to pay twice as much rental in the summer season than in the winter season.

Analysis

Suppose a leasing company is prepared to grant a credit line for $150,000 to the hotel, and would require a nominal rate of return of 10% for six-monthly rentals, i.e. a 5% return every six months.

If we ignore taxation, i.e. the effect of tax allowances on the asset rental the leasing company could quote seasonal rentals to the hotel as follows:

Summer payment	$24,470
Winter payment	$12,235

The summer payment is twice the winter payment and would give the leasing company its desired return. This is illustrated in the table overleaf, showing the present value to the leasing company of the 10 rental payments over the five-year term of the lease.

Season	Year	Payment (in advance)	Discount factor at 5% per six months	Present value of rental
		$		$
Summer	1	24,470	1.0	24,470
Winter	1	12,235	$\frac{1}{(1.05)^1}$	11,652
Summer	2	24,470	$\frac{1}{(1.05)^2}$	22,195
Winter	2	12,235	$\frac{1}{(1.05)^3}$	10,569
Summer	3	24,470	$\frac{1}{(1.05)^4}$	20,131
Winter	3	12,235	$\frac{1}{(1.05)^5}$	9,586
Summer	4	24,470	$\frac{1}{(1.05)^6}$	18,260
Winter	4	12,235	$\frac{1}{(1.05)^7}$	8,695
Summer	5	24,470	$\frac{1}{(1.05)^8}$	16,562
Winter	5	12,235	$\frac{1}{(1.05)^9}$	7,887
				150,007

The present value of the rentals, discounted at a yield of 5% every six months, equals the cost of the investment (with a $7 rounding difference). This shows that the leasing company's return would be 5% every six months, i.e. a nominal return of 10% and an effective rate of 10.25%.

Step-up and Step-down Rentals

A company could expect the income from using an asset to increase over time. It might therefore try to arrange lease finance with stepped payments. Under this type of arrangement, the amount of the rental is increased each year by a given percentage amount or a given money amount, through the primary lease period.

Example

A company wishes to obtain an item of equipment with a full-payout lease. The equipment would cost $76,620. A leasing company is prepared to offer a five-year lease, with rentals payable quarterly in advance.

The company expects the income earned from using the equipment to rise substantially over the next five years, and has asked the leasing company about stepped rentals.

The leasing company would require an investment return of 3% per quarter (a nominal rate of 12% per annum). Taxation and any capital allowance on asset purchases, is ignored for the purpose of this example.

Analysis

If the leasing company quoted a fixed quarterly rental for the full five-year primary lease period, the rental would be $5,000 per quarter, payable in advance.

However, the leasing company might be willing to agree to stepped rentals, with the rental payment increasing by 10% (compound rate) each year. To achieve the leasing company's target return, the payment pattern would be as shown in the table below (workings not shown). This is compared with a fixed rental.

Year	Fixed rental per quarter	Stepped rental per quarter (10% annual increase)
	$	$
1	5,000	4,188
2	5,000	4,607
3	5,000	5,068
4	5,000	5,574
5	5,000	6,132
Total payments (over 5 years)	100,000	102,276

The total payments over the full five-year period are higher for the rising stepped rental lease compared to a fixed rental, to compensate the leasing company for the lower returns in the first years of the lease period.

Deferred Rentals

Some assets do not generate revenue for some time after they have been purchased. A lessee could therefore ask for a rent-free period, i.e. a rental moratorium until such time that the asset is revenue-generating. Rental payments will be higher for leases with a longer moratorium period, to cover the lessor's higher interest cost in providing the asset finance.

Example

A company wishes to acquire some equipment by means of a four-year finance lease. The equipment, costing $250,000, will take up to one year to install and test, and will not become fully operational and revenue-generating for some time.

A leasing company is willing to arrange the lease, and would charge interest at 2% per quarter, i.e. a nominal return of 8% per annum. Rentals would be quarterly, payable in advance. However, the leasing company would be willing to consider a rental moratorium, with no payments for either six or 12 months.

Analysis

The quarterly rental payments will vary according to the length of the rental moratorium, as set out in the table below (workings not shown). Note also how the total rentals payable over the four-year primary period are higher for a longer moratorium.

Length of moratorium	Number of quarterly rentals payable	Amount of each rental	Total rentals over four-year primary period
		$	$
0 months	16	18,052	288,832
6 months	14	21,063	294,882
12 months	12	25,087	301,044

Balloon Payments

Occasionally, a lease could provide for a pattern of rental payments whereby

- the lessee makes regular rental payments throughout the primary period, but these are insufficient for the lessor to recover the full capital cost of the asset
- the lessee makes a lump sum or a balloon rental payment at the end of the primary period, and in doing so enables the lessor to recover the capital cost.

This is illustrated in the graph below.

Ballooned Lease: Lessor's capital recovery

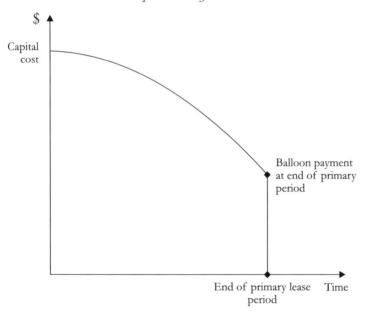

Balloon leases could be appropriate in cases where the asset is expected to have a large residual value at the end of the lease period, but the lessor does not want to bear the residual value risk. A finance lease therefore can provide for a balloon payment at the end of the lease to coincide with the sale of the asset by the lessee, acting as the lessor's selling agent. If the lessor gives most of the proceeds from the sale to the lessee as a rental rebate, the rebate can be set off against the ballooned final payment.

Example
A two-year finance lease for a car provides for eight quarterly rental payments in advance of $1,500 each, and a ballooned payment of $7,500 at the end of the lease period. The lease contract calls for the lessee to sell the car on the lessor's behalf, with all the sale proceeds going to the lessee as a rebate on rental.

Analysis
The lessor will receive eight quarterly rentals of $1,500 and a ballooned payment of $7,500. Because the present value of these payments represents substantially all of the car's fair value at the start of the lease period, the lease is a finance lease.

The lessee receives the sale proceeds from the car after two years. The lessee's final payment to the lessor will be the ballooned payment minus the rental rebate. If the ballooned payment (in this example $7,500) is set at an amount equal to the estimated residual value of the car, the lessee's net payment, if any, should be small

- if the residual value equals $7,500, there will be no net payment by either the lessor or lessee
- if the residual value is less than $7,500, the lessee must pay the shortfall to the lessor
- if the residual value is greater than $7,500, the lessee receives the surplus, with the lessor retaining $7,500 as the ballooned payment.

Small, Middle and Big Ticket Items

Finance leases can be categorized simply according to the value of the leased assets.

Small and Middle Ticket Items

Small ticket leases and middle ticket leases are similar in virtually every respect, except for the asset value. Their main characteristics are

- a primary lease period normally between three and seven years, occasionally longer
- standard lease documentation
- rental payments beginning only after the equipment is delivered to the lessee
- usually fixed lease rentals
- in many cases an early termination clause subject to a termination payment
- in many cases, a requirement for a credit assessment of potential small company lessees.

According to the Equipment Leasing Association (ELA) in the US, a small ticket item is a transaction under $100,000 typically using conditional sales leases or single investor true leases (operating lease). A middle ticket transaction is generally represented by financing under $2 million and dominated by single investor leases. Such a lease is generally a tax-oriented finance lease in which, because of the value of the tax benefit, the rental payments will be lower than for a non-tax based finance lease.

In the UK the value of a small ticket item is generally defined as a transaction between $8,000 and $320,000 and a middle ticket item one that has a value between $320,000 and $25 million.

Big Ticket Items

The ELA also defines a big ticket lease as one dominated by leveraged leases, and represented by lease financing of over $2 million. But many big ticket transactions can be worth $200 million or more, for items such as airplanes, ships and rolling stock.

Most big ticket leases are for large-scale projects and specialized items often costing $200 million or more, such as water treatment plants and oil rigs. The leases can be complex and the documentation is usually specially prepared by lawyers.

Primary lease periods do not exceed the expected useful life of the assets, but can nevertheless be very long, perhaps 10 years, 15 years or even longer.

Lease rentals are usually not fixed, but variable, with interest linked to a benchmark rate such as the London Interbank Offered Rate (LIBOR). Payments are normally made six-monthly or annually, rather than quarterly. Other rental variation clauses could be written into a big ticket lease with a lengthy primary period. For example, a provision normally will be included for the rental to be altered if there is a change in the rate of corporation tax, or if tax rules relating to capital allowances on asset purchases alter.

Small ticket leasing slows down during recessions because most lessees are small to medium enterprises (SME sector) and lessors tend to set higher credit guidelines. Big ticket leasing is usually less affected.

5

Vehicle leasing and contract hire

Car leasing and commercial vehicle leasing make up a large sector of the leasing market. Car dealerships often need financial support to sell their products, and leasing companies provide a variety of finance and leasing products to the vehicle fleet market.

Car Leasing

Lease finance for cars is provided mainly by specialist finance companies. Some are captive organizations of major motor manufacturers including General Motors Acceptance Corporation, Ford Motor Credit, and Chrysler etc.. Others are subsidiaries of banks or other finance companies or specialist vehicle leasing companies, such as Wheels Inc. in the US. Among the largest vehicle leasing companies in the world are GE Capital Fleet Services and Lease Plan International that is headquartered in The Netherlands and owned by the international bank, ABN-Amro. Globally too, an association of premier fleet management and leasing companies has been formed called Interleasing.

Both operating leases and finance leases are widely used for cars. Operating leases usually take the form of contract hire and are described in later chapters.

In the US, Australia and Italy, finance leases for automobiles normally are for four years. In the UK normally they have an initial rental period of two or three years. At the end of this time, the resale value could be around 30% to 40% of original cost. Many finance leases for vehicles therefore are arranged with a balloon rental payment pattern, with

- a fairly low rental cost payable over the initial lease period, covering the fall in the capital value of the car
- a final balloon rental payment at the end of the initial period, equal to the anticipated disposal value of the car at that time.

In Italy lease payments must be spread equally over the lease period, and balloon payments are not permitted.

A finance lease gives the lessee the fleet management responsibilities for negotiating the purchase with the dealer, arranging to pay insurance and tax costs as well as servicing and repairs.

At the end of the lease period, the lessee either can hand the vehicle back to the lessor who will sell it, or he may set about selling it himself. For example, a lessee in the UK usually acts as the lessor's agent in selling the vehicle, perhaps as a trade-in for a new one from a dealer and the lessee retains most of the sale proceeds. The lessee's share of the sale proceeds can be set off against the final balloon rental payment on the lease. If the proceeds are less than the balloon rental, the lessee must pay the difference.

A finance lease for an automobile often will allow the lessee to continue to use the car beyond the initial lease period, paying the same amount of periodic rental, rate or perhaps a slightly lower instead of paying the balloon rental. This type of lease is an open-ended lease that gives the lessee flexibility in deciding when to dispose of the vehicle(s). But the lessee also guarantees that the lessor will realize a minimum value from the sale of the asset at the end of the lease.

Selling Automobile Leases

Vehicle leasing is sold both by motor dealers who have perhaps arranged a sales and leasing plan with a finance company, and by the leasing companies themselves. Banks with a leasing subsidiary could encourage local managers to cross-sell the bank's services, and suggest leasing to a corporate customer when the opportunity arises in the business relationship. The leasing subsidiary also will employ its own specific marketing methods.

The target market for automobile leasing consists mainly of

- companies with large fleets of vehicles
- companies looking for ways of avoiding capital outlays and preserving cash
- vehicle dealers and suppliers that could improve their sales by offering lease finance to customers (vendor or sales-aid leasing).

Contract Hire

Operating a large and complex fleet of vehicles is not usually part of a company's core business. As a consequence, most companies do not have the resources to manage their vehicles efficiently, or do not recognize the need to invest in fleet management, even though large expenditures are incurred every year on vehicle running costs.

Contract hire is a form of operating lease for motor vehicles. It has evolved as a method of providing

- lease finance, together with
- improvements in fleet management and cost control.

Unlike a standard vehicle lease, contract hire is an operating lease where the lessor, not the lessee, arranges for the acquisition and eventual disposal of the vehicles, as well as providing the lease finance. In addition, the lessor usually will provide a range of fleet management services for the lessee, and take over the day-to-day tasks of managing the company's vehicles.

The fleet management services provided by the lessor can be tailored to the lessee's requirements, but can include

- vehicle servicing and repairs
- obtaining vehicle road tax
- providing replacement vehicles for vehicles that are off the road for lengthy repairs
- providing a roadside assistance and recovery service
- providing management and fleet performance information.

If the lessor in a contract hire agreement agrees to obtain car insurance and provide fuel for the lessee, these are invariably charged for separately on an actual-cost basis.

In a full-service contract-hire agreement, all the lessee has to do is specify the type and number of cars he wants, the required lease period and the expected number of miles/kilometers of travel over the lease period. All the administrative tasks of obtaining and operating the car fleet are taken on by the lessor.

Development of Contract Hire

Contract hire developed in the US throughout the 1980s as competitive pressure forced lessors to find new ways to compete. Favorable tax regulations on company vehicles also helped. Success in the US meant the concept of contract hire started to take off in the UK and, at a slower rate, across the rest of Europe.

The large volume of leasing business associated with these fleets encouraged lessors to develop fleet management services. This development improved the appeal of contract hire in other European countries where company fleets tend to be smaller than in the UK. Many companies liked the idea of handing fleet management responsibilities to a specialist external organization, i.e. the contract hire company.

Cost of Contract Hire

The contract hire company (lessor) must quote a price for its service. The price will depend on the services required by the lessee and the estimated costs, and will include

- vehicle purchase costs
- finance charges
- estimated maintenance and administration costs
- minus the estimated residual values, based on the lease period and the estimated distance of travel.

These costs are converted into a fixed periodic rental, e.g. a guaranteed monthly rental. The lessee has no further costs to pay, except that if the vehicles travel greater distances than estimated, a premium could be payable. The leasing company bears all the risks that running costs could be higher than expected, or residual values lower.

Advantages of Contract Hire

The advantages to the lessee of contract hire can be substantial.

- Off-loading administrative tasks. Fleet management is the responsibility of the lessor's experienced staff. Customers do not have to spend time and effort on the non-core activity of fleet management, and could avoid the need to hire a full-time manager for the fleet.
- Cost control. Contract hire rentals are fixed. Budgeting can be more exact, and better cost control is achievable.
- Cost efficiency. The lessor can provide economies of scale in purchasing, fleet management, IT support and disposal. Such cost efficiencies can be passed on to the lessee. For example, a leasing company, as a bulk buyer of vehicles for contract hire, can often negotiate large purchase discounts for its customers.
- Financial reporting. The vehicles, being acquired under an operating lease, are not shown as fixed assets in the lessee's balance sheet. Contract hire is a form of off balance sheet finance.
- Avoiding capital expenditure. As with other types of lease finance, contract hire avoids the need for a company to use up capital for asset purchases.

Contract Purchase

Contract purchase is similar to contract hire, except that the customer has the option to buy the vehicles at the end of the contract. This makes contract purchase similar to hire purchase. It was developed in the UK as a method of improving the size of allowances that a contract hire customer can claim against tax. UK tax law limits the amount of the finance element in vehicle lease rentals that is allowable for tax purposes.

6

Vendor Leasing

Vendor leasing, also known as vendor programs and sales aid leasing, is a specialized form of leasing in which a customer is offered lease finance as part of the sales package. The sales representatives of the equipment supplier offer the option of lease finance to potential customers as a means of stimulating sales, i.e. lease finance is part of the marketing of the supplier's product, and is therefore an aid to selling. Potential customers are given an opportunity to obtain a new asset without having to incur any capital expenditure. The standard leasing documentation can be handled by the supplier's salesperson, so that for the customer, obtaining the equipment and obtaining lease finance are combined into a single purchasing process.

Vendor leasing is mainly used for small ticket items that are sold to a wide customer base, such as office equipment, office furniture, photocopiers, communications equipment, motor cars and printing machines. However, there are some sales and leasing schemes for middle ticket items such as computer equipment, and big ticket items. Vendor leasing can be available for both finance and operating leases.

Lease finance is just one element of the supplier's marketing mix, and vendor leasing is often combined with a very flexible approach to selling including deals on discounts, trade-ins, upgrades and termination options, and a strong brand image for the product.

The Leasing Company

The supplier could have its own leasing subsidiary to provide the lease finance. Alternatively, the supplier can make an arrangement with a separate leasing company, either directly or through a broker, for the provision of lease finance to creditworthy customers.

Example
A manufacturer of vending machines could be having difficulty selling its machines to customers, who do not have the money to buy them. The manufacturer might reach an agreement with a finance company to offer lease finance to creditworthy customers, enabling them to acquire vending machines from the manufacturer's range of models. Finance could be bundled with the supply of consumables as a complete facilities package.

Analysis
The vending machine salesperson could offer an operating lease to potential customers, and handle the documentation for the customer's application for lease finance. Subject to credit approval by the finance company, the lease can be quickly arranged.

- The vending machine will be sold to the leasing company and hired out to the customer.
- The supplier receives payment for the sale from the leasing company.
- The customer receives delivery of the vending machine, and is able to rent the machine rather than buy it. The lease agreement could include an option for early termination or an upgrade to a more expensive type of machine.

In an arrangement between an equipment supplier and a finance company, the supplier has to be aware of the finance company's concerns about creditworthiness. Although leasing can be a sales aid for the supplier, it cannot be offered indiscriminately to all potential customers. There must be a clear message that lease finance will be available only with credit approval.

In addition, since much vendor leasing involves operational leases, the finance company will expect the leased items to retain their value, and have a well-established secondhand market; otherwise the residual value risk will be too high.

Lessor Requirements

A leasing company providing vendor leasing schemes for equipment manufacturers (or distributors) should be expected to provide technical and administrative support to the manufacturer or distributor to make the scheme work efficiently. The required support facilities are listed.

Support Facilities Required
- Nationwide availability to back up the supplier's national sales force
- Speedy credit vetting and response to applications for lease finance from the supplier's customers
- Easy-to-complete and easy-to-understand lease documentation
- Rate cards, specialized calculators or PC software for the supplier's sales force, for quoting lease rental rates for set rental periods
- Training the supplier's sales force to understand aspects of leasing
- Efficient administrative procedures for the prompt payment of suppliers on receipt of properly completed lease documentation and delivery of the equipment to the customer
- Information and procedures to record the equipment on lease to assist with future sales initiatives and upgrade programs.

Buy-Back Agreements

The supplier of equipment and the leasing company could very well include a buy-back agreement, or a remarketing agreement, in their vendor leasing scheme.

If a lessee defaults, the supplier could buy back the equipment from the lessor at a guaranteed price, and resell it on the secondhand market. This arrangement would give some added protection to the leasing company against credit risk.

A buy-back agreement could also apply to the disposal of the equipment at the end of the primary lease period. The supplier will then buy back the equipment and resell it in the secondhand market.

A potential advantage for the supplier from a buy-back arrangement or remarketing agreement is the ability to exercise some control over the secondhand market for its products. Because buy-backs often constitute contingent liabilities for suppliers, they usually seek a form of remarketing agreement that could not be construed as a formal commitment.

Potential Problems with Vendor Leasing

Although most vendor leasing schemes have operated well, some schemes have attracted criticism. These are set out below.

Many of these alleged abuses could be the result of high-pressure sales techniques. Some photocopier salesmen, for example, have been accused in the past of persuading customers to lease photocopiers that are too large for their requirements, under a cost-per-copy agreement that is also subject to a minimum rental payment. Customers are then committed to a series of high minimum rental payments because their use of the photocopier is relatively low, and their rental charge on a cost-per-copy basis is never sufficient to reach the minimum rental amount.

A further problem can arise out of upgrading schemes, where the customer (lessee) is given the option to terminate a lease agreement provided he takes on a new lease for new equipment. The termination payment could then be rolled up into the cost of the new equipment, and the lessee pays rentals on the inflated price. When the lessor is asked to fund a leased asset at an inflated price, the quality of its security, that is the value of the equipment, is diminished.

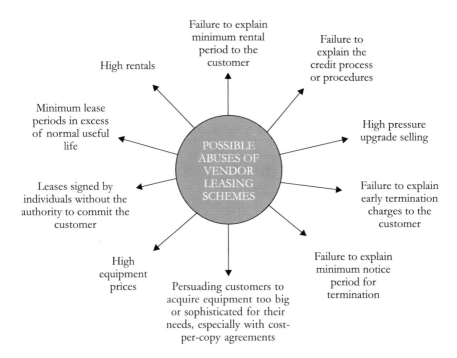

Failure to explain minimum rental period to the customer

Failure to explain the credit process or procedures

High rentals

Minimum lease periods in excess of normal useful life

High pressure upgrade selling

POSSIBLE ABUSES OF VENDOR LEASING SCHEMES

Leases signed by individuals without the authority to commit the customer

Failure to explain early termination charges to the customer

High equipment prices

Failure to explain minimum notice period for termination

Persuading customers to acquire equipment too big or sophisticated for their needs, especially with cost-per-copy agreements

Example

An equipment supplier has a vendor leasing arrangement. It sells two models of equipment, costing $20,000 and $30,000 respectively. A customer acquires a $20,000 model under a three-year lease, and the lease provides for an early termination payment by the lessee. If the customer terminates the lease after 18 months, say, the termination payment would be $8,000.

However, the equipment supplier would be willing to roll up the termination payment into the cost of a new model, provided the customer upgrades from the $20,000 to the $30,000 model.

Analysis

If the customer terminates the old lease after 18 months and upgrades to the higher-priced model, the purchase cost on which the lease rental payments are based will be $38,000. This comprises the fair value of $30,000 plus the termination payment of $8,000, rolled up into the cost of the new model.

The leasing company will be asked to provide asset finance for $38,000, but will have an asset with a fair value of just $30,000 as security for its lending. The customer, on the other hand, focuses on the cost per month rather than the renewed three-year commitment.

7

Arranging a Lease

Bank loans are a traditional form of medium-term asset finance, and businesses are often more likely to consider a bank loan to finance an asset purchase than leasing. The creation of new leasing business depends on bringing potential lessees into contact with potential lessors, and then agreeing terms for a lease.

Preliminary Approach

The preliminary approach for arranging lease finance could come from the prospective lessee, a lease broker, or from the leasing company's marketing staff.

The decision by a company to obtain lease finance will depend on

- the willingness of a leasing company to provide the finance, and
- the cost of leasing, compared to buying.

Leasing companies will need information about

- the type of equipment involved, its delivery date and location
- the estimated cost of the equipment
- the desired primary lease period
- if appropriate, the tailored rental pattern required by the customer
- financial details about the customer.

Supplied with this information, a leasing company can assess the potential lessee's creditworthiness and judge whether it would be willing to provide the lease finance. The leasing company also will have to decide what profit margin it would require in order to quote rental terms. The financial evaluation of a lease by a lessor is described in more detail in Chapter 10.

Because rental terms will vary between leasing companies, the prospective lessee should ask for an indication of the size of rental from a number of leasing companies. Alternatively, a broker can be asked to obtain rental terms from a number of leasing companies, and to give advice on which terms are the best. The broker's fees usually are paid by the lessee, but can be paid by the lessor by adding them to the amount of lease finance provided, and on which rentals the lessee will pay.

Selling Leasing

Leasing companies will try to win business by approaching suitable companies and asking about their potential interest in lease finance. The methods of identifying companies to approach, as well as making an approach, vary according to circumstances.

- Where the leasing company is the subsidiary of a bank, the bank's client liaison officers or relationship managers could be asked to identify potential leasing customers.
- Potential customers with whom the leasing company has no previous connection can be identified from business directories, referrals from business contacts or similar sources.

The type of company to be approached as a potential leasing customer will be determined by the leasing company's marketing plan. For example, the marketing team could be given a brief to identify those companies that

- are likely to operate a sizable fleet of motor vehicles
- are in an industry where technology is important
- have fairly low profitability, and could be unable to utilize all their tax allowances for asset purchases
- are subsidiaries of foreign parents that may not be earning

sufficient profits to utilize tax allowances in full
- are expanding rapidly
- are likely to want to fix the cost of their assets over their useful life and might prefer fixed asset rentals to a purchase financed by a variable rate loan. These companies include small capital-intensive businesses such as printing firms.

An approach to a potential leasing customer is more likely to be well received when there has been a previous business relationship. In this respect, the value of a banking relationship can be invaluable, with the bank's liaison officer for a corporate client acting as the point of contact.

For many leasing companies, however, marketing involves a large amount of regular cold calling by telephone, backed up perhaps by direct mail.

The Lease Contract

Leases normally are between a leasing company and a commercial user of income-producing assets. Leases to consumers, as distinct from short-term rental agreements, are uncommon. Although leases can be tailored to the individual requirements of the lessee, the contract must always include certain terms and conditions, relating to

- the identity of the lessor and the lessee
- the asset (or assets) being leased
- the lease period
- the rental payments
- maintenance of the asset
- the return or disposal of the asset at the end of the lease
- use of the asset
- insurance of the asset
- early termination of the lease
- taxation provisions and corporate taxes.

Selling lease finance

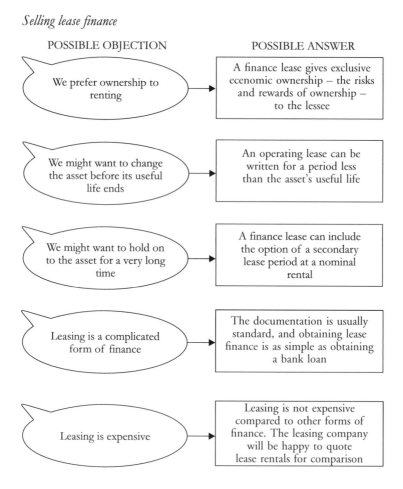

POSSIBLE OBJECTION	POSSIBLE ANSWER
We prefer ownership to renting	A finance lease gives exclusive economic ownership – the risks and rewards of ownership – to the lessee
We might want to change the asset before its useful life ends	An operating lease can be written for a period less than the asset's useful life
We might want to hold on to the asset for a very long time	A finance lease can include the option of a secondary lease period at a nominal rental
Leasing is a complicated form of finance	The documentation is usually standard, and obtaining lease finance is as simple as obtaining a bank loan
Leasing is expensive	Leasing is not expensive compared to other forms of finance. The leasing company will be happy to quote lease rentals for comparison

Often there also will be conditions relating to rental adjustments. The contents of a typical lease agreement are illustrated below.

Finance Lease Documentation

1 Identity of the lessee and the lessor (owner)
2 Lease commencement date. Balance outstanding; formula to determine the amount owed by the lessee if termination were to occur. Interest rate chargeable on overdue payments
3 Identification of the goods; the leased assets and their location. Lease period, primary plus secondary. Primary period

4 Rent. Secondary period
5 Lessee's undertaking to pay rentals promptly and in full. Interest to be payable on overdue rentals. Owner has the right to add sales tax to the rental, at the current rate of tax
6 Lessee accepts responsibility for choosing the asset, taking delivery, installation, operation and use. Owner (lessor) not liable for any claims for losses through injury etc. arising from use of the asset. Lessee responsible for maintenance and repairs
7 Lessee responsible for risks arising from loss, theft or destruction of the goods. The owner has full right over the goods
8 Lessee's undertakings include using the goods in accordance with manufacturer's recommendations, and using them only for their designed purpose and in a proper manner, and not to remove the goods from the address stated in the lease, etc.
9 Lessee's undertakings include ensuring that the goods at all times comply with legal requirements, not taking the asset out of the country; affixing a nameplate to the asset showing ownership
10 Lessee's undertakings include reimbursing the owner for expenses incurred in protecting his interests in the goods; surrendering the assets on termination of the lease; and indemnifying the owner against all claims by third parties arising from use of the goods.
11 Insurance. Terms and conditions of insurance requirement set out, including the lessee to pay all premiums; the owner to receive the proceeds from any insurance claim; the owner to be the person to agree or make any settlement of a claim
12 Representations and warranties by the lessee
13 Termination of the lease. Conditions under which the lessor can terminate the lease, for example non-payment of rental, insolvency of the lessee
14 Right of the owner to take possession of the goods if the lease is terminated. Termination payment. The amount of the termination payment set out in detail
15 Termination payment. Voluntary termination
16 Return of goods at end of lease. Right of the owner to appoint the lessee to sell the goods as the owner's agent. Agreement of the owner to pay a rental rebate to the lessee if the lessee sells the asset as the

owner's agent

17 Rental adjustments. Circumstances under which the rental payments will be altered. Giving the lessee notice of rental changes

18 General terms and conditions. Signed by the owner and the lessee, and witnessed. Applicable law. Methods of giving notice and the assumed delivery periods for each.

For many small and medium ticket items, standard lease documentation can be used to make the process of arranging the lease both quicker and much cheaper.

When a company leases equipment regularly from a leasing company, a master leasing agreement can be prepared, and subsequent leases of individual assets are all covered by the terms and conditions of the master lease.

Other documents required by the leasing company could include acceptance certificates to prove delivery and installation, personal or corporate guarantees, waivers (mortgagees or landlords), remarketing or repurchase agreements for the supplier or manufacturer and documents to substantiate the authenticity of the signatory.

Agency Arrangements

If a company regularly acquires assets under lease agreements, it could enter into formal agency arrangements with a number of leasing companies. Under such an arrangement, the company would act as agent for the leasing company, with authority to negotiate the purchase of assets from a supplier and perhaps also to pay for them. Alternatively, the supplier can be asked to send the invoice to the lessor. In its role as the lessor's agent, the company in fact obtains ownership for the lessor, not for itself.

This type of arrangement can be convenient because it can speed up the process of obtaining new assets, and yet avoids the complication of the prospective lessee first buying the asset himself and having to pass legal title to the leasing company in order to arrange the lease.

- The lessee can negotiate the purchase of the asset with the supplier, knowing that finance will be available to pay for it.
- There is never any requirement for ownership to pass from the company (as initial buyer) to the leasing company, under a sale and leaseback or a novation arrangement.
- Administration can be reduced. One payment stream can cover several asset purchases.

Agency agreements can be either informal and unwritten, or strictly formal and carefully written out.

8

Taxation Issues

While the treatment of leases and leased assets for tax purposes varies between different countries, the basic issues are similar.

The basic tax issues to consider are

- the taxation of lease rentals for the lessor and the allowable costs of rentals for the lessee, and
- capital allowances, that is the tax rules that apply to the purchase cost and residual sale value of the leased asset.

Lease Rentals

For the lessor, lease rentals represent taxable income. For the lessee, lease rentals are generally deductible from taxable profits.

In the US most states have a single sales/use/rental tax on the leasing of equipment. States with these taxes require that the leasing company report and remit tax on the gross rents billed or collected from their respective lessees. Exemptions are possible and there are many rules relating to this.

Capital Allowances

A capital asset has an expected useful life of several years, but is paid for in full at purchase. The purchase cost of the asset (for the lessor) is an allowable cost for tax purposes, it can be set off against taxable profits;

however this capital allowance must be spread over the useful life of the asset, and usually cannot be allowed in full in the year of purchase. This tax rule is widely applied by countries throughout the world, although in some cases a 100% allowance for the full purchase cost of an asset could be granted to the purchaser in the year of purchase.

Capital allowances therefore are applied on principles similar to the depreciation of fixed assets in financial accounting, where the cost of an asset is spread over its expected life.

In some countries, such as Germany, the capital allowance for tax purposes is the same as the depreciation charge in the financial accounts. In countries such as the US and UK, companies can decide their own rates of depreciation for financial reporting, but separate rates for capital allowances are applied under tax regulations, i.e. depreciation charges and capital allowances are different amounts.

The capital allowances available each year for the cost of an asset purchase usually will vary according to the type of asset. If, for example, there is a 25% tax depreciation charge (MARCS), this means that the capital allowance each year is 25% of the written down value of the asset. The written down value is the cost of the asset minus the cumulative capital allowances claimed to date.

For an individual item of plant or machinery costing $1,000, the annual capital allowance and written down value of the asset are shown in the table overleaf.

With a system of 25% writing down allowances, about 90% of the original purchase cost of the asset has been allowed against tax in the first eight years of the asset's life.

Capital allowances usually can be set off against taxable income in computing the company's liability to corporation tax. The cash benefit from the allowance therefore depends on the rate of tax. If the tax rate is 50%, a capital allowance of $200 is worth $100 in tax saved. If the tax rate is only 30%, a capital allowance of $200 will save just $60.

Year	Opening value	Capital allowance (25%)	Written down value
	$	$	$
1	1,000.00	250.00	750.00
2	750.00	187.50	562.50
3	562.50	140.62	421.88
4	421.88	105.47	316.41
5	316.41	79.10	237.31
6	237.31	59.33	177.98
7	177.98	44.50	133.48
8	133.48	33.37	100.11
9	100.11	etc.	

Taxation on Asset Disposals

When the asset is eventually sold or scrapped, there could be a further tax charge relating to the difference between the asset's written down value at the time of sale and the sale value.

Example

An asset costing $10,000 was sold by a company for $2,500 after five years, when its written down value was $2,373. The rate of corporation tax is 30%.

Analysis

The sale value is $2,500, but the asset's written down value is lower. The company is therefore subject to a balancing charge, as follows:

	$
Sales value	2,500
Written down value	2,373
Balancing charge	127

The total allowances for the asset over the period are $7,500 that is the difference between its purchase cost of $10,000 and its sale price of $2,500. This results in total tax charges of $2,250 (30% of $7,500). The benefits are spread over time as follows:

73

Year	Capital allowance		Tax saved at 30% (9 months after year-end)
	$		$
1	2,500		750
2	1,875		563
3	1,406		422
4	1,055		316
5	791		237
	7,627		2,288
6 (charge)	-127	(x30%)	-38
Total	7,500		2,250

Pooling System

In some countries, the system of capital allowances, or their equivalent, requires a separate record to be maintained of the written down/depreciated value for each individual asset. Capital allowances are calculated for each asset individually.

In other countries, a pooling system operates. A company maintains a pool of assets on which allowances can be claimed. The value of the pool is the original cost of the assets, less the allowances previously deducted. A writing down allowance is applied to the pool as a whole.

The capital allowance for a company's pool of assets might, for example, be calculated as follows. Illustrative figures are shown.

		$
	Pool as at the start of the year	1,000,000
Minus	Sale proceeds of assets sold in the year, or their cost, if this is a lower amount	-120,000
		880,000
Add	Cost of assets purchased in the year	180,000
		1,060,000
Minus	Writing down allowances, i.e. capital allowances, at 25%	-265,000
	Pool carried forward to the next year	795,000

Under the pooling system sometimes there can be a slightly different treatment of outstanding written down values when an asset finally comes to be sold.

- If the sale value on disposal is higher than the outstanding written down value, the excess is subject to tax.
- If the sale value on disposal is less than the outstanding written down value, the surplus WDV is retained in the pool of written down values, and allowances must continue to be claimed at the appropriate annual rate.

Capital Allowances and Leasing

Capital allowances are granted to the owner of the asset. For a leased asset, this is the lessor. The lessee cannot claim capital allowances, but can claim the cost of lease rentals against taxable income.

Tax rules help to distinguish leasing from hire purchase. Hire purchase requires the user, the eventual owner, not the provider of finance, to claim the capital allowances on the asset. With hire purchase, the payment installments from the buyer to the provider of finance are considered similar to loan repayments, consisting partly of a capital repayment and partly of interest. Only the interest element in the hire purchase payments is taxable income for the finance provider and an allowable expense against tax for the user.

Tax Benefits of Leasing

Leasing can have a tax benefit for either the lessee or the lessor. When the lessor benefits, some of the gain can be passed to the lessee in the form of lower lease rentals.

The benefits are greater when capital allowances can be claimed sooner rather than later. For example, suppose than an asset costs $1 million, and the purchase cost attracts capital allowances. If there is a 100% capital allowance in the year of purchase, the full cost of the asset can be claimed against tax immediately. If the capital allowance is spread over a number of years, the tax benefits will also be spread out and its net present value reduced. The tax benefits of leasing therefore depend on the length of time the asset buyer has to wait before the full purchase cost can be set off against tax.

Leasing can provide tax benefits, compared with outright purchase of the asset, for any of the following reasons

- rentals are allowable costs against taxable income
- the lessee could have registered insufficient profits to claim all the due allowances
- the lessee's rate of tax is lower than the lessor's
- the lessor's tax year ends at a more advantageous time than the lessee's, with respect to the date of asset purchase.

Rentals Allowable Against Taxable Income

The lessee's rental costs are usually allowable in full against taxable income. This often means that the lessee can write off the cost of the asset against tax more quickly than if the asset had been purchased.

Example

An asset costing $40,000 is leased for four years under a finance lease agreement. The lessee intends to continue using the asset beyond the primary lease period. If purchased with a bank loan, the asset would attract writing down allowances of 25% per annum.

Analysis

If the asset is leased, the company will claim the rental charges as allowable expenses each year for four years. The rental charges represent the lessor's capital recovery plus interest on the finance. The company therefore will claim the full cost of the capital cost plus interest charges against taxable profits.

If the asset is purchased with a bank loan, the loan interest will be an allowable expense. Over a four-year period, however, capital allowances will cover less than 70% of the asset's cost.

In this situation, leasing could provide cash flow benefits to the company acquiring the equipment, compared to purchasing, by accelerating the timing of the expenses allowable against tax.

Sufficiency of Profits

A company buying equipment can claim the capital allowances itself. However, if it has no taxable profits, it cannot claim the capital allowances. Similarly, if it has capital allowances in excess of its taxable profits, the allowances cannot be claimed in full. The allowances can often be held over until taxable profits are earned, but the benefit will nevertheless be delayed.

In this situation, leasing can provide lower cost finance to the lessee. The finance company (the lessor) can take the allowance at the earliest time permitted, and pass on some of the benefit in lower lease rentals. For the lessee, leasing can be a cheaper method of financing the asset than purchasing with delayed capital allowances.

Example

Two companies, Alpha and Beta, each have taxable profits, against which the current year's capital allowances can be claimed, of $800,000. In the same year, both companies buy assets costing $1 million.

The pool of unrelieved capital allowances on assets, excluding the new purchases, is $2 million for Alpha and $3 million for Beta. Writing down allowances are 25% per annum. Tax is 30% of taxable profits.

Analysis

Alpha can claim the full amount of capital allowances on the assets it purchased in the year, but Beta cannot. This is illustrated in the table on the next page.

	Alpha	Beta
	$	$
Original pool of assets	2,000,000	3,000,000
New purchases	1,000,000	1,000,000
	3,000,000	4,000,000
Writing down allowance permitted (25%)	750,000	1,000,000
Taxable profits	800,000	800,000
Writing down allowance claimed (limited by taxable profits)	750,000	800,000
Writing down allowance carried forward	-	200,000

Alpha can claim all its capital allowance entitlement in the current year, whereas Beta must defer $200,000 of allowances until at least the next year. With tax levied at 30% for example, Beta must defer $60,000 of tax savings until it has earned sufficient taxable profits to claim the available allowance.

In this situation, leasing assets could be more attractive to Beta than to Alpha, because the buy alternative does not offer the same cash flow benefits that Alpha can obtain. In other words, leasing can be more tax efficient for Beta than for Alpha.

Lessee's Tax Rate

In countries where smaller companies are taxed at a lower rate than large companies, the tax benefits from buying an asset are bigger for large companies. For example, if large companies are taxed at 30% and small companies at 20%, the tax benefit of a capital allowance of $1,000 is $300 for a large company but only $200 for a small company.

Provided that lease finance is available at a competitive rate to small companies, leasing can be cheaper than buying an asset.

Tax Year-End

The first writing down allowance on equipment can be claimed for the year when the equipment is purchased, regardless of the date of purchase during the year. If corporation tax is payable in the nine months after the end of the tax year, this means that if a company's year ends on December 31, tax for the year is payable on the following October 1. If the company buys an asset for $100,000 on January 2 and another asset, also for $100,000, on December 31, the 25% capital allowance can be claimed on both ($25,000 for each asset) and this will result in a lower tax payment on the following October 1. For the asset purchased on January 2, the tax benefit occurs 21 months later. For the asset purchased on December 31, the tax benefit occurs just nine months later.

The greatest cash flow benefit therefore is obtained by purchasing assets as close to the year-end date as possible, by minimizing the delay until the tax benefit is earned. But in the US provisions have been brought in to prevent loading assets into the last half of the year as well as a basic tax called Alternative Minimum Tax that can affect a lessor's tax position.

Changing the pattern of allowances alters the relative benefits of leasing and purchasing for the lessee since the tax benefits to the lessor have been reduced. The lessee may need to look at a lease versus purchase analysis as described in the next chapter.

Significance of Tax for the Leasing Industry

The growth of leasing in the US in the 1950s and in the UK in the 1970s was stimulated by tax legislation. In the US a system of accelerated tax depreciation, i.e. capital allowances on equipment began in 1954. The benefits were further enhanced in 1961 by investment tax credits (ITC). An ITC was an allowance against tax payable rather than against taxable income. The favorable tax treatment for capital investment in plant and machinery was largely brought to an end in 1986 with the passage of the Tax Reform Act.

In the UK, a new system of capital allowances was introduced from 1972, whereby the purchase cost of plant and equipment qualified for a 100% tax allowance in the year of purchase, a 100% first-year allowance. The tax benefit was therefore accelerated, full allowance given in the first year rather than spread over the asset's life. At about the same time, the rate of corporation tax for larger companies rose to 50%, thereby increasing the potential cash flow benefits of accelerated tax allowances.

The new capital allowance system coincided with a period of low corporate profitability, but rapid inflation. As a consequence, many companies did not earn enough profits to claim first-year capital allowances in full. Finance companies, notably banks, were able to offer leasing as a lower-cost method of asset finance because

- as lessors, they could benefit from the accelerated capital allowances, and pass on some of this benefit to the lessee in the form of a lower rental, and
- lessees were able to claim the full rental cost against tax.

Equipment for leasing could be purchased by a subsidiary in the finance group. If a lessee company had chosen to purchase its own assets instead of leasing them, usually it would be unable to claim the tax benefit quite so quickly.

The UK tax rules for capital allowances changed in 1984 with effect from 1986, and 100% first-year allowances were scrapped. At the same time, corporation tax rates were reduced. It was widely believed at the time that the leasing industry would contract because tax advantages had been reduced. Against all expectations, leasing business continued to grow. Similar views were expressed in 1997 following the curtailing of the first-year allowances available to lessors.

Conclusion

The tax aspects of leasing affect the cash flows of the lessor and the lessee. They are important

- for the lessee, in deciding whether to lease or buy outright, and
- for the lessor, in deciding the rental that should be charged to earn a satisfactory after-tax profit and return on investment.

These issues are explored in the following chapters.

9

The Lease: The Asset Finance Decision

When a business considers acquiring an item of equipment, there is a two-stage decision process. These stages are

- the investment decision
- the financing decision.

The investment decision is whether or not the business should acquire the item. This is a commercial decision, related to why the equipment is needed, and what the expected benefits from having it would be. Reasons for wanting the equipment could be to replace items that have reached the end of their useful life, to develop a new product, to cut running costs, or to install new equipment required by law in order to meet environmental or health and safety regulations.

Once the commercial decision has been taken to acquire the equipment, the next stage is to decide how the acquisition should be financed.

The Investment Decision

Deciding whether to acquire an item of equipment is a commercial matter for the business concerned, and is largely beyond the scope of this book. If the equipment is expected to earn income for the business, factors in the investment decision will be

- the purchase cost of the equipment
- tax relief on the purchase cost
- the anticipated operational cash flows, that is cash profits from

The decision process

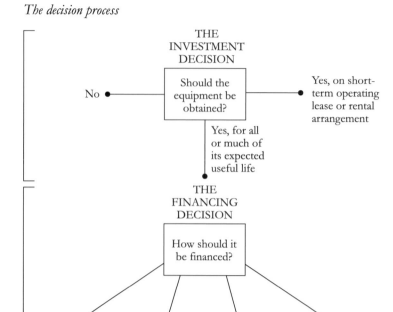

using the equipment, net of tax payments

- the equipment's expected residual value, if any, at the end of its useful life.

If the benefits appear to exceed the costs, investing in the equipment would be justified.

If the equipment is not expected to generate income for the business, the investment decision could depend on whether the expected costs of acquiring and using it are justified by the intangible benefits.

Businesses have their own methods of reaching investment decisions, and such methods vary in the degree of financial sophistication. For substantial investments it is recommended that the evaluation should be based on

- an assumption that the equipment, if acquired, will be purchased

- a discounted cash flow (DCF) analysis of the expected costs and benefits.

The Financing Decision

Once a business decides to invest in an item of equipment and becomes its economic owner, it should then consider how the acquisition might be financed.

Most financing options involve either the immediate or eventual purchase of the equipment. An immediate purchase can be financed out of existing cash resources by raising the money from a bank loan, or by issuing new shares or bonds. Deferred purchase can be arranged through hire purchase or installment credit. For all these options, the business user of the equipment is entitled to the capital allowances that the equipment attracts under tax regulations. In contrast, if the equipment is obtained by means of a lease, the capital allowances are claimed by the lessor, not the lessee, the equipment user.

Period of Use – Buy or Rent?

If a business expects to use the equipment for most of its useful life, it almost certainly will be cheaper to acquire economic ownership through purchase or a finance lease rather than through a short-term operating lease or rental agreement.

If the equipment will be required for less than its expected life, a business could consider purchase in preference to an operating lease or rental. However, if the equipment is purchased, the business will expect to resell it when it is no longer required, and the overall cost of the equipment purchase will depend on the resale price obtained. When there is some doubt about the likely residual value of the equipment, purchase could be a high-cost option. With some items of equipment, such as automobiles, the secondhand market could be liquid, and resale prices fairly predictable. Purchase with the intention of resale could then be a valid alternative to rental or operational leasing.

The Cost Factor in Lease vs Buy

Choosing the appropriate way of financing an asset will often depend on the relative costs of each available method. This cost comparison is often referred to as the lease versus buy decision, but it can also include different methods of purchase, such as rental or conditional sale known as hire purchase.

Comparative Cash Flows in the Lease vs Buy Decision

Because the commercial decision to invest in the asset has already been taken, the operational cash flows that are anticipated from using the asset are irrelevant to the financing decision and so can be completely ignored. These cash flows include sales income generated from asset use, as well as operating costs.

A comparison of the different financing options for an asset should focus on the cash flows that will arise as a direct consequence of the method selected. They are shown below.

Purchase (cash resources)	Purchase (bank loan)	Conditional sale or hire purchase	Finance lease
Purchase cost (finance outlay)	Loan repayments (capital and interest)	Payment installments (capital and interest)	Lease rentals
Tax relief from capital allowances	Tax relief on interest payment	Tax relief from capital allowances	Tax relief on rental payments
Residual value at end of life (if any)	Tax relief from capital allowances	Tax relief on interest element in payments	Rental rebate at end of lease period, if the asset is sold by the lessee as agent for the lessor
	Residual value at end of life (if any)	Residual value at end of life (if any)	

The Interest Cost of the Buy Option

There is an interest cost for each of the financing methods involving asset purchase. If an asset is purchased with money from a bank loan, the interest cost is the rate of interest on the loan, adjusted to allow for tax relief on interest payments. Broadly, this means that if the rate of interest on a loan is 10% and the rate of corporation tax is 30%, the net-of-tax (after-tax) cost of the loan finance will be 7% (10% less 30% of 10%).

If an asset is purchased with the internal cash resources of the business, the interest cost is the opportunity cost of the income forgone by using the cash to buy the asset instead of using it for other purposes, e.g. paying a dividend to shareholders.

For the purpose of evaluating a purchase option, compared to a finance lease option, it is often assumed that the asset user would have to borrow the money to pay for the purchase. The comparison of the lease or buy options is therefore

- purchase of the asset with a bank loan, and
- a finance lease.

The Discount Rate for a Lease vs Buy Comparison

The costs of leasing over the useful life of the asset can be compared with the costs of asset purchase. Because the cash flows stretch over a number of years, they should be discounted to a present value for comparative purposes. The cheaper financing method is the one with the lowest present value of cost after tax.

The discount rate selected for converting future cash flows to a present value is the interest cost of borrowing. This could be a marginal cost of funds, internal hurdle rate or the weighted average cost of capital.

With a purchase option, one of the cash flow items is the loan payment schedule. No matter what the loan payment schedule is, the present value of the loan cost is simply the amount of the loan. A feature of borrowing is that if the loan repayments, including interest charges, are discounted to a present value at the interest cost of borrowing, their present value must equal the amount of the loan.

It might help to illustrate this point mathematically.

Example
A company borrows $100,000 at 10% per annum for four years. The loan repayments are $10,000 per annum in interest charges, payable annually, and a lump sum capital repayment of $100,000 after four years. Interest payments are an allowable expense for tax purposes, and tax is payable at 30% on profits.

Analysis
The cost of loan interest should allow for the tax relief on interest payments. If it is assumed, for simplicity, that tax payments arise in the same year as the interest charges, the after-tax cost of interest is

$$r(1 - t)$$

where r is the gross (pre-tax) interest cost and t is the rate of tax as a proportion (e.g. 30% = 0.30).

In this example, the after-tax cost of interest would be 7.0% (10% x [1 - 0.30]).

The present value of the loan repayments, allowing for the tax relief on interest and discounted at a rate of 7.0% is $100,000.

This is shown in the table overleaf.

However, tax is saved only when the tax payment becomes due. This could occur some time after the interest payments giving rise to the tax relief. The correct after-tax cost of a loan depends on how long after the interest payments the benefits of the tax saving will be earned. In the example above, suppose that tax relief on interest payments is earned 12 months after the payments are made. The after-tax cost of the loan would then be about 7.2%, because this is the rate of discount at which the loan payments have a present value of

Year	Interest/ capital payment	Tax relief on interest charge at 30%	Net cash flow	Discount factor at 7.0% per annum	Present value
	$	$	$		$
1	10,000	(3,000)	7,000	$\dfrac{1}{1.07}$	6,542
2	10,000	(3,000)	7,000	$\dfrac{1}{(1.07)^2}$	6,114
3	10,000	(3,000)	7,000	$\dfrac{1}{(1.07)^3}$	5,714
4	10,000	(3,000)	7,000	$\dfrac{1}{(1.07)^4}$	5,340
4	100,000		100,000	$\dfrac{1}{(1.07)^4}$	<u>76,289</u>
					100,000

$100,000 (allowing for approximation error). This is illustrated in the following table.

Year	Interest/ capital payment	Tax relief on interest charge at 30%	Net cash flow	Discount factor at 7.2% per annum	Present value
	$	$	$		$
1	10,000		10,000	$\dfrac{1}{1.072}$	9,328
2	10,000	(3,000)	7,000	$\dfrac{1}{(1.072)^2}$	6,091
3	10,000	(3,000)	7,000	$\dfrac{1}{(1.07)^3}$	5,682
4	10,000	(3,000)	7,000	$\dfrac{1}{(1.07)^4}$	5,300
4	100,000		100,000	$\dfrac{1}{(1.07)^4}$	75,721
5	(3,000)		(3,000)	$\dfrac{1}{(1.07)^5}$	<u>(2,119)</u>
					100,003

The longer the period of delay between incurring interest charges and earning tax relief, i.e. the date of the tax payment against which the tax allowance can be claimed, the higher will be the after-tax cost of capital.

At this stage the important point to understand is that if loan repayments are discounted at their after-tax cost of interest, the present value of the repayments equals the amount of the loan. In a lease-versus-buy comparison, the cost of purchasing an asset with a bank loan is compared to the cost of leasing. The financial cash flows are converted to a present value, using the after-tax cost of the loan as the discount rate. In the case of the buy-with-loan option, the present value of the loan payments and offsetting tax relief will equal the purchase cost of the loan.

This means that the present value of the loan-purchase option is simply

- the cost of the asset, with adjustments for the tax relief from the capital allowances on the cost of the asset, and
- the residual value of the asset (if any) at the end of its life.

The Lease vs Buy Evaluation Method

To compare the cost of an option to buy an asset financed by a bank loan, with an option to lease, the cash flows that should be compared are as follows:

Buy	Lease
Purchase cost (present value of loan)	Lease rentals
Tax savings through capital allowances	Tax relief on lease rentals
Residual value (if any)	Rent rebate on resale (if any)

The cash flows or the costs of each option should be discounted at the after-tax cost of borrowing. The cheaper financing option is the one with the lower present value of cost.

Example
A company has decided to acquire an item of machinery costing $200,000. This could be purchased either, with money from a bank loan, or leased for five years.

If the machinery is purchased

- it would attract capital allowances of 25% each year on the written down value
- it is expected that the machinery would be used for five years and then sold for $50,000
- interest on the loan would be 10% per annum.

If the machinery is leased

- it would be sold for an estimated $50,000 by the lessee at the end of the primary lease period. The lessee would act as agent for the lessor, and receive 95% of the sale price as a rent rebate at the end of Year 5
- lease payments would be $47,000 each year, payable annually in advance.

The rate of corporation tax is 30%. It can be assumed that any tax payments or tax savings will occur 12 months after the event, giving rise to a taxable charge or tax allowance.

Analysis

For the purpose of clarity, some of the assumptions in this example have been simplified. Lease payments are annual, rather than quarterly or six-monthly, and tax savings or tax charges occur exactly 12 months after the corresponding event that gives rise to a tax allowance or taxable income. Simplifying the timing of cash flows means that an annual rate of discount can be applied to calculate the present value of the cash flows.

When cash flows occur at irregular intervals throughout the year, it would be necessary to convert an annual discount rate into a six-monthly, quarterly or even daily rate of discount if a high degree of accuracy should be required.

In practice, companies that use the discounted cash flow (DCF) method to compare the costs of financing options (lease versus buy) generally will make some simplifying assumptions, and in doing so avoid complexities in the evaluation.

If the machinery is purchased, the user will obtain capital allowances. These can be calculated as follows

Year	Written-down value (WDV)	Tax allowance (25% of WDV)	Tax saving at 30% (1 year later)
	$	$	$
0	200,000	50,000	15,000
1	150,000	37,500	11,250
2	112,500	28,125	8,438
3	84,375	21,094	6,328
4	63,281	15,820	4,746
5	47,461		

At the end of the fifth year, the equipment will be sold for $50,000. This will give rise to a taxable charge because the sale value is higher than the written down value at the time of sale.

	$
Sale price	50,000
WDV	47,461
Taxable charge	2,539
Tax at 30%	762

The loan repayments can be ignored because the cash flows will be discounted at the after-tax cost of the loan. This is 7.0% (10% less 30% of 10%). The present value of the loan repayments (capital and interest) is the amount of the loan, or the purchase cost of the machinery.

If the machinery is leased, the relevant cash flows are the lease rentals, tax relief on these rentals, reducing the tax payable one year later, the rental rebate at the end of the primary lease and tax on the rebate.

DCF evaluation should establish the present value of the cost of the buy and the lease options respectively. The cheaper option is the one with the lower present value of cost.

Purchase Option: Present Value of Cost

Year	Item	Amount	Discount factor at 7.0% per annum	Present value
		$		$
0	Cost of loan	(200,000)	1.0	(200,000)
1	Tax saved (Capital Allowance)	15,000	$\dfrac{1}{1.07}$	14,019
2	Tax saved	11,250	$\dfrac{1}{(1.07)^2}$	9,826
3	Tax saved	8,437	$\dfrac{1}{(1.07)^3}$	6,888
4	Tax saved	6,328	$\dfrac{1}{(1.07)^4}$	4,828
5	Tax saved	4,746	$\dfrac{1}{(1.07)^5}$	3,384
5	Sale value	50,000	$\dfrac{1}{(1.07)^5}$	35,649
6	Tax payment (surplus on sale)	(762)	$\dfrac{1}{(1.07)^6}$	(508)
				(125,914)

In this example, the leasing option is slightly cheaper than the purchase option. However, the difference in cost is not large, and the company's decision to lease or buy could therefore be influenced by factors other than cost.

It is also important to recognize that the cost comparisons are based on certain assumptions that could in the event turn out to be incorrect. In this example, important assumptions are that

- the sale value of the machinery after five years will be $50,000
- the rate of corporation tax will remain at 30%, and the rules on capital allowances will not change
- the loan would be at a fixed 10% rate of interest; therefore there would be no upward or downward movement in loan interest costs if the machinery were purchased.

Lease Option: Present Value of Cost

Year	Item	Amount	Net cash flow	Discount factor at 7.0% per annum	Present value
		$	$		$
0	Lease payment (in advance)	(47,000)	(47,000)	1 .0	(47,000)
1	Tax relief (30%)	14,100			
1	Lease payment	(47,000)	(32,900)	$\frac{1}{(1.07)^1}$	(30,748)
2	Tax relief	14,100			
2	Lease payment	(47,000)	(32,900)	$\frac{1}{(1.07)^2}$	(28,736)
3	Tax relief	14,100			
3	Lease payment	(47,000)	(32,900)	$\frac{1}{(1.07)^3}$	(26,856)
4	Tax relief	14,100			
4	Lease payment	(47,000)	(32,900)	$\frac{1}{(1.07)^4}$	(25,099)
5	Tax relief	14,100	14,100	$\frac{1}{(1.07)^5}$	10,053
5	Rent rebate (95% of $50,000)	47,500	47,500	$\frac{1}{(1.07)^5}$	33,867
6	Tax on rebate (30% of $50,000)	(15,000)	(15,000)	$\frac{1}{(1.07)^6}$	(9,995)
					(124,514)

Tax Position of the Lessee

In the previous example, it was assumed that the company considering whether to lease or buy machinery would be able to claim all the available tax relief at the earliest opportunity. This presupposes that the company is earning sufficient taxable profits against which allowances in fact may be claimed.

If the company is in a different tax position; for example, if it expects to make losses for the next few years, evaluating the lease or buy decision should be based on different assumptions. In particular, it would be inappropriate to use an after-tax cost of capital as the discount rate during the period when the company will not be earning taxable profits. During this period, the cost of new asset finance to the company will be the pre-tax, i.e. gross, cost of the finance, since tax relief cannot be claimed until taxable profits are earned.

For companies in this situation

- there will be a greater reluctance to invest in new assets, because the cost of acquiring the assets will not be offset by tax allowances until the company starts to earn profits again
- if a decision to invest in a new asset is taken, and both leasing and purchase with a bank loan are available options, an evaluation of the financing options should be certain to take the expected tax position into consideration

Conclusion

Leasing can be an attractive additional source of finance to a business seeking to acquire new assets. The cost of leasing must be competitive, and the costs of different methods of finance should be compared. In practice, the most sophisticated method of evaluation for comparing lease and buy options uses discounted cash flow analysis. Most businesses using the DCF technique will make certain simplifying assumptions, and remove unnecessary complexities from their evaluation.

Leasing companies, in contrast, are finance companies that are in business to make satisfactory profits from the leases they sell. Leasing must be competitively priced to win customers, but must also earn a profit. The financial evaluation of leases for the lessor is therefore crucially important, and complex evaluation methods are necessary for leasing companies. These are discussed in the next chapter.

10

The Lessor: Lease Finance

A lessor aims to make a profit out of providing asset finance. The concerns of the lessor are therefore related to

- what the lease rentals must be to recover the capital invested by the lessor in the lease and earn a suitable profit
- where appropriate, the residual value of the asset
- the creditworthiness of the lessee, and
- how the lessor's position can be protected against unpredictable events, such as a change in interest rates (and the lessor's cost of funds), a change in the tax rules, or the desire of the lessee to terminate the lease early.

Recovery of Capital Investment

With a finance lease, the lessor expects to recover all the capital cost, or substantially all of the cost, from rentals received in the primary period of the lease. Where the full cost of the investment is recovered from rentals, the lessor's capital investment in a finance lease will diminish over the primary lease period

- from the amount of finance provided at the start of the lease period
- to zero, at or soon after the end of the lease period.

Example
A lessor provides finance for a five-year lease. The full capital amount will be recovered from rentals over this primary period. The cost of the asset purchase is $100,000 and lease rentals are $7,000 quarterly, payable in advance.

Analysis

The lessor's investment in the lease will be $93,000 at the start of the primary lease period.

	$
Asset cost	100,000
Less first rental paid in advance	7,000
Initial investment	93,000

At the end of the primary lease period, the investment in the lease should be close to, but not exactly zero. This is because there will still be a further tax payment or a tax saving for the lessor, arising out of the lease rentals and capital allowances. When the tax position is eventually settled, the lessor's investment in the lease will be zero, i.e. the full capital cost will have been recovered.

Profit on a Lease

A lessor expects to make substantially all his profit on a finance lease from the rentals received from the lessee. If the asset has no residual value to the lessor, the profit over the lease period will be the total rentals minus the cost of the asset, adjusted to allow for

- the finance cost of the lessor's investment, and
- taxation.

Total Profit

Total profit for a finance lease over the full period of the lease can be tabulated as follows:

Income (+) or Savings (+)	Expenditure (-)
Lease rentals	Tax on lease rentals
Tax saved on capital allowances for asset purchase cost	Asset purchase cost
Lessor's share of residual value	Tax on lessor's share of residual value
Reduction in tax due to interest cost of finance being tax allowable	Interest cost of finance

Spreading the Profit Over the Lease Period

The lessor must also decide how the total profit from a lease should be spread over each of the years of the lease. The method of attributing profit to leases can vary between different leasing companies. A method commonly used is the actuarial method. This method is based on the assumptions that

- profit is removed from the lease by means of an actual or notional dividend distribution, over the primary lease period
- the amount of profit removed each year will provide a constant rate of return on the lessor's average net cash investment in the lease during the year, throughout the primary lease period.

In other words, the lessor's return on net investment is a constant percentage amount for every year of the lease. The profit per year therefore diminishes over the lease period, as the lessor's net investment falls to zero.

In practice, a leasing company will use a computer program to calculate what the rentals should be to achieve the target profit or rate of return on the lease. A variety of factors affect the lease rental or lease profit. These will include

- the length of the lease and number of rental payments
- the lease start date (date in the tax year)
- the leasing company's year-end

- capital allowances
- the rate of corporation tax
- the interest cost of funds
- the reinvestment rate for surplus funds.

The following example illustrates the basic principles of lease financing from the lessor's viewpoint. It is intended to show the financing and tax cash flows that the lessor must consider. *NB The example is used for illustrative purposes only and is not based on actual tax rates that vary widely from state to state.*

Example

A leasing company's financial year ends on December 31. It pays corporation tax on annual profits nine months after the year-end, on October 1.

It arranges to lease an item of equipment on December 31, Year 1. The lease has a five-year primary period and rentals are $25,400 per year, payable annually in advance.

The equipment will attract capital allowances of 25% each year on its written down value. Corporation tax is 30%.

At the end of the primary lease period, the equipment will be sold, with all the sale proceeds going to the lessee as a rent rebate.

The leasing company pays interest on its funds. Interest, which is at an annual rate of 11%, is calculated on the daily balance of funds borrowed, and is payable annually on December 31.

Profits will be withdrawn from the lease on an actuarial basis. The rate of profit is 1.425% per annum of the average investment in the lease.

If there are any surplus funds relating to the investment in the lease, the leasing company can reinvest them to earn just 3% per annum interest.

Analysis

To avoid excessive complexity, the calculations in this example have been simplified. In particular, the tax implications beyond Year 7 are ignored. In practice, there would be tax relief on the interest paid in Year 7, receivable in Year 8.

The cash flows the lessor will consider are

- the amount of finance provided
- tax saved due to the capital allowances
- lease rentals
- tax payable on the lease rentals
- interest on the lessor's net investment in the lease
- tax relief on the interest cost.

A summary of the cash flows is shown in the table below. The total profit on the lease is as follows

	$	$
Lease rentals (25,400 x 5)		127,000
Tax on rentals (at 30%)		-38,100
		88,900
Capital cost	-100,000	
Tax allowances (at 30%)	30,000	
		-70,000
		18,900
Interest cost of finance	-22,400	
Less tax saved	6,720	
		-15,680
Income after tax		3,220

The total profit of $3,220 is spread over the lease period, as shown in the following table, to give a return on net investment of 1.410% per annum.

Lease – Cash Flows and Profits

Year	WDV	Calc. WDA	Tax Saved	Rental payments	Tax on rent	Interest	Tax relief on interest	After tax profit	Net invest- ment
	$	$	$	$	$	$	$	$	$
1	(100,000)	-		25,400		-	-	1,067	(76,118)
2 (1.10)	(99,932)	(68)	20		(7,620)	(8,206)	-	945	(67,469)
(31.12)				25,400					
3 (1.10)	(74,949)	(24,983)	7,495		(7,620)	(6,365)	2,462	653	(46,750)
(31.12)				25,400					
4 (1.10)	(56,211)	(18,737)	5,621		(7,620)	(4,321)	1,910	362	(26,122)
(31.12)				25,400					
5 (1.10	(42,159)	(14,053)	4,216		(7,620)	(2,309)	1,296	67	(5,206)
(31.12)				25,400					
6 (1.10)	(31,619)	(10,540)	3,162		(7,620)	(262)	693	126	(9,360)
(31.12)									
7 1/10	(23,714)	(31,619)	9,486		-	(937)	79	-	(732)
8 1/10	(17,786)	-	-		-		281	-	0
	(100,000)	(100,000)	30,000	127,000	(38,100)	(22,400)	6,720	3,220	0

The net investment should reduce to $0 at the end of the lease as above.

The workings are explained in the tables overleaf.

Capital Allowances

The capital allowance claimed each year results in a tax saving on October 1 in the following year.

Year (Dec 31)	Allowance	Written-down value
	$	$
1	* 68	99,932
2	24,983	74,949
3	18,737	56,211
4	14,053	42,159
5	10,540	31,619
6	31,619	0

* The allowance in year-one is calculated as 1/365 x $25,000 = $68

Year (Dec 31)	Allowance	Tax saving (30%)
	$	$
1	68	20
2	24,983	7,495
3	18,737	5,621
4	14,053	4,216
5	10,540	3,162
6	31,619	9,486
	100,000	30,000

Tax on Rentals

Rentals of $25,400 each year, payable on December 31, will attract tax at 30% ($7,620). The tax is payable on the following October 1.

Interest on the Net Investment

Interest at 11% is payable annually on December 31. For the purposes of the evaluation, the interest is charged on the average investment in the year.

Year	Net investment	Interest at 11%
	$	$
2	74,600	8,206
3	57,867	6,365
4	39,281	4,321
5	20,989	2,309
6	2,379	262
7	8,521	937
Total		22,400

Net Investment and Annual Profit

Profit is calculated on an actuarial basis, and is taken out of the lease each year at a constant annual percentage return (in this example at 1.410%) of the net investment at the year-end. The computation of annual profit is a painstaking process if done manually, but can be done very quickly by computer.

The net investment consists of:

	$
Purchase cost of the asset	A
Minus tax saved from capital allowances	- B
Minus rentals received	- C
Plus tax on rentals	+ D
Plus interest cost on investment*	+ E
Minus tax relief on interest*	- F
Plus profit withdrawn	+ G

$$A - B - C + D + E - F + G$$

Or minus interest receivable on surplus, less tax on the interest.

Year	Net investment at year-end	Profit at 1.410% per annum
	$	$
2	75,667	1,067
3	67,018	945
4	46,299	653
5	25,672	362
6	4,755	67
7	8,908	126
	281	
Total		3,220

Risks for the Lessor

The previous example, showing the lessor's cash flows for a finance lease, can help to illustrate some of the risks facing the lessor. By looking at the cash flows, and seeing in particular how interest costs are calculated, it can be seen how profits can be affected by interest rates, the timing of cash flows and tax rates. Factors that could impair the profitability of a lease include

- late payment (or non-payment) of rentals by the lessee
- an increase in the lessor's cost of funds
- a fall in the lessor's reinvestment rate for earning interest on surplus funds
- changes in taxation rules and rates
- a lower-than-expected residual value
- legal claims against the lessor by a third party.

Credit Risk

The lessor is exposed to the risk of non-payment or late payment of rentals by the lessee. The risk can be reduced by a credit appraisal of potential lessees, and by refusing leases to customers that seem an unacceptably high risk; nevertheless, some risk is unavoidable.

It is helpful to understand the consequences to the lessor of late rental payments. The cash flow profile in our example on page 115 shows that interest costs are a significant cash flow for the lessor. Delays in the receipt of rentals will increase the lessor's interest costs because the net investment in the lease is reduced when a rental payment is received and late payments therefore reduce the profitability of the lease. In cases of long payment delays, the lessor could even make a loss on the lease.

Cost of Lease Funds

The lessor usually must obtain funds from external sources to provide asset finance to lessees. When the leasing company obtains its funds from variable rate borrowing, it is exposed to the risk of an increase in interest rates. When interest rates go up, the cost of the leasing company's funding increases and the interest costs of its individual contracts will also rise.

In our example the lessor assumed that the cost of funds would be 11% per annum for the duration of the lease. If this assumption were to be incorrect, the profit on the lease would be higher if the interest rate fell below 11%, and lower if the interest rate went up.

A leasing company can try to ensure a profit on its leases by fixing the cost of its funds. The sources of lease funding, and methods of fixing the cost of funds, are described later in this chapter.

Interest Variation

Most small and middle ticket finance leases are on fixed rentals. Some leases, particularly for big ticket items, provide for variations in rental payments when interest rates alter. However, even when a lease has fixed rental payments, a provision can be included for interest rate changes.

- Rentals may be fixed in relation to the level of interest rates as at the date of purchasing the equipment, i.e. the date on which the lessee draws down the finance from the lessor. Until the asset is purchased and the interest rate is established, the rental is not fixed.
- A provision could be included for rentals to be increased or

reduced by a specified amount for each 1% change in the level of interest rates over the primary lease period.

A condition in a lease could provide for a periodic adjustment to the rental, to allow for the difference between the actual rate of interest and the rate of interest initially assumed for the purpose of calculating the lease rental. These adjustments could be made annually, semi-annually or quarterly, in arrears.

Reinvestment Rate Assumption

In most lease evaluations, there will be a period, usually towards the end of the lease, when the lessor has over-recovered the capital outlay, and there is a surplus of funds rather than a net investment in the lease. The surplus is eventually eliminated by further tax payments. An assumption is made by the lessor at the start of the lease about what the reinvestment rate will be for surplus funds. This is the rate at which the lessor will earn interest on the temporary funds surplus, and add to the profit on the lease. If the reinvestment rate is lower than anticipated, the profit also will be less.

Tax Changes

The terms for a tax-based finance lease are arranged on the basis of existing tax rules. A change in the rate of taxation, or a change in the rules applying to capital allowances, could affect the profitability of the lease. Our previous example should make this clear. A change in the rate of taxation, for instance, would alter the lessor's tax payments (on rentals) and tax relief (on capital allowances and interest costs). The profitability of the lease also will change.

Tax Variation

Just as a lease can provide for changes in interest rates over the lease period, it can also provide for rentals to be adjusted in the event of changes in

- the rate of corporation tax
- the rate at which capital allowances can be claimed
- the system of capital allowances.

Residual Value Insurance

When the lessor expects a leased asset to have some residual value at the end of the lease period, e.g. with operating leases, there could be a risk that the actual residual value will be less than originally expected. A condition of most leases is that the lessee should maintain the asset in good working condition that is essential to sustain its value. The lessee is also liable for any loss or damage to the asset, and returning it in the stipulated condition, fair wear and tear excepted.

A lessor can sometimes obtain insurance protection against loss resulting from the residual value of an asset being less than the amount expected when the lease was written. The insurance, known as residual value insurance or asset value insurance, covers the lessor for the difference between a pre-agreed estimated residual value and the actual value at a specified future date.

Residual value insurance is suitable for assets that are unlikely to become obsolete and unsellable. Examples are ships and aircraft. It is also used with some computer leasing to construct true operating leases, but it is very expensive.

Risk of Third Party Claims

A lessee could use a leased asset

- for an illegal purpose
- for a purpose other than the one for which it was intended, or
- without proper regard to the manufacturer's operating instructions.

As a result, there could be injury or damage to property, resulting in a third party claim against the lessee and the lessor.

The lease contract will require the lessee to obtain suitable and adequate insurance against material damage and for third party risks. Should the insurance cover be insufficient, however, the lessor could be required to meet any demand for compensation that the lessee is unable or unwilling to pay.

For example in November 1993 EuroAir, a Portuguese regional airline, sued British Aerospace, the airplane manufacturer, and CIBC Finance plc, lease financiers to EuroAir for three BAe aircraft. EuroAir sued for $70 million, claiming breach of contract and recurrent defects in the three airplanes. Earlier in the year, CIBC Finance had repossessed the airplanes from EuroAir and claimed that EuroAir owed it over $37 million.

Failure to Recover the Asset

Although the lessee is contractually obliged to return the asset at the end of the lease period, there can be occasions when the lessor is unable to recover it. If the asset has a residual value, the potential loss to the lessor could be high, and legal action to recover the asset might be necessary.

A complex legal issue can arise if a lessee attaches the leased equipment to property. The equipment can then become a fixture and can be claimed by the owner of the real estate. It is therefore usual for the lessee to covenant in the lease agreement that he will not attach the equipment to land or premises so that it becomes a fixture. Lessors sometimes insist on a landlord's waiver so that the property owner acknowledges the lessor's interest in the equipment on commencement of the lease.

Lease Finance

A leasing company, like a bank, obtains most of its funds from external sources and uses them to provide finance to customers (lessees). Most funds are obtained from money market term loans, up to two years. Longer term (variable rate) loans are also used.

Leasing companies normally will use a variety of funding sources. Large finance companies can issue debt securities, such as bonds or commercial paper (CP). Commercial paper has the advantage of flexibility because the issuer can vary the amount of paper in issue to match its need for funds. There have also been some issues of asset-backed securities, where the asset backing is provided by leased assets, e.g. leased computers.

Interest Rate Risk

Leasing companies, like banks, are exposed to significant interest rate risk. A finance company makes a profit from the difference between the cost of borrowing and the income from relending. Risk arises from the volatility of interest rates, so that the cost of borrowing can be higher than expected, or the income from lending less than expected.

Mismatch Risk

Mismatch risk occurs when a leasing company's borrowings mature at a different time to the termination of its leases. Mismatch risk is illustrated in the following diagram.

Mismatch risk

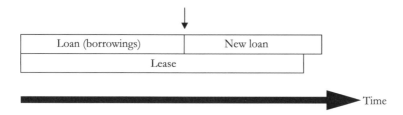

If a leasing company has borrowed funds and the loan matures before the end of the lease that the loan has financed, the company will obtain a new loan to continue the funding. If interest rates have gone up, the cost of new borrowing will be higher, but the income from the lease will be unchanged unless an interest rate variation clause has been written into the lease.

Basis Risk

Basis risk occurs when the interest on borrowed funds is charged on one interest rate basis, e.g. a commercial paper rate, but the interest charge built into lease rentals is on a different basis, e.g. the three-month London Interbank Offered Rate. One interest rate can alter without a corresponding change in the other, thereby affecting the lessor's profit on the lease.

Hedging Interest Rate Exposures

Exposures to interest rate risk can be hedged by a leasing company, if required, by fixing the cost of borrowed funds. A variety of instruments are available for organizations that borrow at a variable rate allowing them either to fix or to set a maximum limit to the cost of borrowing over a specified period. These instruments include forward rate agreements (FRAs), interest rate futures, interest rate swaps and interest rate options, including interest rate caps.

Interest rate risk, and instruments of hedging risk, are covered in *Interest Rate Risk Management*, another of the series in the Financial Risk Management program.

11

Accounting for Leases

It is useful to consider the accounting aspects of leasing, both for the lessee and the lessor. Financial reporting requirements vary to some extent between countries, although there is also a large degree of similarity. US reporting requirements will be used to explain the accounting issues involved, and comparisons will be made with UK and international accounting standards.

Lessee Accounting

Accounting for leases in the US is broadly similar to UK practice, and is based on the same accounting principles. There are, however, some differences of detail, notably

- the rules for distinguishing between a finance lease, often referred to as a capital lease in the US, and an operating lease, and
- the method(s) used by the lessor to allocate gross earnings to individual years of the lease period.

For example, FAS 13 (the Statement of Financial Accounting Standards No. 13), the UK equivalent is SSAP21, uses a four-point test to distinguish capital leases from operating leases. If the answer is yes to any of the following, then the lease is a capital lease for classification purposes.

- automatic title transfer on expiry
- bargain purchase option available to the lessee
- lease period greater than 75% of the asset's economic life
- present value of the minimum lease payments greater than 90% of the fair market value of the asset.

Until the introduction of FAS 13 in November 1976 leasing was often referred to as off-balance sheet financing. This statement required that certain leases be recorded on the lessee's balance sheet as a liability and the leased property reported as a fixed asset. This procedure is called lease capitalization and forms the basis of much of the lease accounting legislation around the world. For leases that fail to meet the test specified by FAS 13 the lessee need only disclose certain information regarding lease commitments in a footnote. At the start of the finance lease, the asset in the balance sheet is matched by a liability to the lessor, i.e. an obligation to pay future rentals.

The standard originally was based on the concept of substance over form. This means

- legal ownership of leased assets belongs to the lessor
- but the effective economic ownership of a leased asset, with a finance lease, belongs to the lessee.

Under FAS 13, the value of the leased asset and the obligation to the lessor (the matching liability) should represent the present value of the minimum lease payments, derived by discounting these payments at the rate of interest implicit in the lease. In practice, a valuation based on the fair value of the asset is usually an acceptable equivalent.

Often lessees prefer a lease to be classified as an operating lease for financial reporting purposes.

Example
A company obtains an asset under a five-year finance lease agreement. Total rentals payable over the five years will be $90,000. The fair value of the asset is its purchase cost of $75,000.

Analysis
If the company prepared a balance sheet at the start of the finance lease, it would include the following items:

	$
Fixed asset	75,000
Liability to lessor	75,000

The difference of $15,000 between the fair value of the asset ($75,000) and total rentals payable ($90,000) represents payments of interest.

The leased asset, recorded as a fixed asset in the lessee's accounts, should be depreciated in the same way as any other fixed asset.

Lease Rentals

The lease rental payable each year should be divided into two parts

- a payment of part of the obligation to the lessor, i.e. a capital repayment, and
- a finance charge, i.e. interest charge. The total finance charge payable under a lease should be apportioned between each accounting year of the lease term to provide a constant annual rate of interest per annum on the balance of the lessee's remaining obligation to the lessor.

Example

A five-year capital lease begins on January 1 Year 1. The annual rental is $5,000, payable in advance. The fair value of the asset is $20,500 and it is expected to have a residual value of $4,863 at the end of the lease period. This is equal to its tax written down value at that time, and the residual value will be paid over to the lessee as a rebate of rentals. The lessor must therefore recover the full capital cost of $20,500 from the lease rentals. The finance charge implicit in the lease is 11.04% per annum.

Analysis

The total lease rentals will be $25,000 ($5,000 per annum x 5 years) and the fair value of the asset is $20,500. The finance charge over the five-year lease period is therefore $4,500 ($25,000 - $20,500).

Using an actuarial basis for calculating interest, the finance charge will be spread over each of the five years as shown in the table below.

Year	Out-standing	Rental	Capital sum during the year	Interest at 11.04%	Capital sum at end of year
	$	$	$	$	$
1	20,500	5,000	15,500	1,711	17,211
2	17,211	5,000	12,211	1,348	13,559
3	13,559	5,000	8,559	945	9,504
4	9,504	5,000	4,504	496	5,000
5	5,000	5,000	0	0	0
				4,500	

The capital sum at the end of the year is the amount at which the outstanding obligation to the lessor should be reported as a liability in the lessee's balance sheet.

The annual rentals will be divided between finance charge and capital repayment as follows:

Year	Finance charge	Capital repayment	Total rental
	$	$	$
1	1,711	3,289	5,000
2	1,348	3,652	5,000
3	945	4,055	5,000
4	496	4,504	5,000
5	0	5,000	5,000
	4,500	20,500	25,000

Operating Leases

Operating leases should be accounted for differently. In the accounts of the lessee, operating lease rentals payable should be recorded as an expense over the lease term as they become payable. The leased item is not recorded as an asset in the lessee's balance sheet. Reporting operating leases is therefore very different from reporting capital leases. Although neither the leased asset nor the obligation appears in the balance sheet, the lessee must disclose the following information in the footnotes to its financial statements: (1) a general description of the leasing arrangements that would include such things as the existence of renewal or purchase options and escalation clauses; (2) the lease expense for each year in which the income statement is presented. A clear distinction between the two types of asset therefore is required. (3) future minimum lease payments required in the aggregate and separately for each of the next five years.

The 90% Test

FAS 13 defines a finance lease as "a lease that transfers substantially all the risks and rewards of ownership of an asset to the lessee". It should be presumed that this transfer occurs if, at the beginning of the lease period, the present value of the minimum lease rentals, including any rental payable in advance, amounts to substantially all of the fair value of the asset. The present value is calculated by discounting the minimum rental payments at the interest rate implicit in the lease. "Substantially all" means 90% or more; hence this guideline in FAS 13 is referred to as the 90% test.

Lessor Accounting

The requirements for financial reporting by lessors differ between finance leases and operating leases.

Finance (Capital) Leases

In the US, FASB 13 requires a lessor's interest in a finance lease to be shown in the balance sheet as a debtor, not as a fixed asset. The lease, in substance, represents a future stream of rental income. The value at which the debtor should be shown is the amount of the lessor's net investment in the lease.

Total (gross) earnings from a finance lease, over the full lease period, are the total rentals receivable, plus any residual value for the lessor, minus the cost (fair value) of the asset. For example, suppose that annual rentals for a five-year finance lease are $3,000 and the fair cost of the asset is $14,000. The gross earnings over the five-year period are $1,000 ($3,000 per annum x 5 years minus $14,000). Gross earnings are profits before deducting the lessor's interest costs and tax on the profit on the lease. Total gross earnings should be allocated to each year of the lease, i.e. the profit should be spread over the period of the lease. FASB 13 requires that the total pre-tax profit should normally be allocated to each year of the lease to give a constant annual return on the lessor's net cash investment in the lease.

Example

A leasing company arranges a five-year lease on an item of equipment. The fair value of the equipment is $20,000 and the rental is $5,200 per annum, payable annually in advance. At the end of the lease, the asset will be sold by the lessee on behalf of the lessor, and the full residual value will be paid to the lessee as a rebate on rental.

The company has analyzed the annual rentals into gross earnings and debt recovery as follows:

Year	Total rental	Gross earnings (before interest and tax)	Reduction in net investment
	$	$	$
1	5,200	2,243	2,957
2	5,200	1,795	3,406
3	5,200	1,278	3,921
4	5,200	684	4,516
5	5,200	0	5,200
		6,000	20,000

This allocation of gross earnings over the lease period will give a constant return per annum on the lessor's net cash investment in the lease.

Analysis

The leasing company would report the gross profit (gross earnings) for each year of the lease as shown in the table on page 116.

The balance sheet at the end of each year will include an item for the lessee's future debt obligations.

Year	Calculation	Balance sheet debtor
	$	$
1	20,000-2,957	17,043
2	17,043-3,406	13,637
3	13,637-3,921	9,716
4	9,716-4,516	5,200
	5,200	0

Operating Leases

A lessor should report assets leased under operating lease agreements as fixed assets in the balance sheet. Fixed assets should be depreciated to their estimated residual value over their expected useful life.

Rental income from operating leases should be recognized as income over the lease period on a straight-line basis.

Example 1

A two-year operating lease with rentals of $1,000 per quarter excluding service charges, begins mid-way through the lessor's accounting year.

Analysis

The rental income will be attributed to each year as follows:

Year	$
1 (2 quarters)	2,000
2 (4 quarters)	4,000
3 (2 quarters)	2,000
	8,000

Example 2

A three-year operating lease has the following payments pattern (excluding service charges) that includes a balloon payment at the end of the lease.

Year	Rentals
	$
1	2,500
2	2,500
3	10,000
	15,000

Analysis

The rental income should be recognized on a straight-line basis over the three-year period, i.e. as $5,000 per year.

The profit on an operating lease is the rental income, less running costs (service charges, etc.) asset depreciation and interest costs as incurred.

Initial Direct Costs

Initial direct costs of a lease are the costs incurred by the lessor in negotiating and arranging the lease. These can include a broker's commission, legal fees, the cost of a credit check on the lessee and the costs of preparing the lease documentation. The lessor either can charge these initial direct costs immediately against profits or spread them over the term of the lease.

Operating Leases and Residual Values

The reported profit on an operating lease depends on the depreciation that the lessor charges for the asset. The depreciation charge in turn depends on the estimated residual value of the asset.

Example

An asset costing $50,000 has an estimated useful life of six years and an estimated residual value of $14,000 after six years. It is leased for two years at an annual rental of $7,200.

Analysis

The lessor could charge depreciation of $6,000 per annum on the asset.

	$
Cost	50,000
Estimated residual value	14,000
Depreciable amount	36,000
Annual depreciation ($36,000 ÷ 6 years)	$6,000

The annual gross profit on the lease, measured as rental income less depreciation, therefore will be $1,200 ($7,200 - $6,000).

However, the lessor might have over-estimated the residual value of the asset. If so, the annual profits will be over-estimated. The losses eventually will become apparent when the assets are disposed of. For example, suppose that the actual residual value at the end of six years is just $2,000, not $14,000. The depreciable amount of the asset should have been $48,000 and the annual depreciation charge should have been $8,000 ($48,000 ÷ 6 years). Instead of making a profit of $1,200 per annum on the lease, there would have been a loss of $800 per annum. The lessor's over-estimate of profit eventually will become apparent when the asset is sold for less that its book value.

The Case History of Atlantic Computers

The importance of residual values for profits on operating leases was evident in the collapse of the computer leasing company, Atlantic Computers in 1990.

With operating leases, the lessor takes a risk on the residual value of the equipment. For this reason, operating leases have been less common than finance leases for many types of asset. Operating leases have been widely used, however, for computer leasing. During the 1960s, a secondhand market developed in the US for IBM 360 series mainframe computers. As a result, secondhand values for IBM equipment became reasonably predictable, and computer leasing grew rapidly. Some leasing companies specialized in computer leasing.

In 1970, IBM introduced the 370 series of computers, replacing the 360 series, whose secondhand values consequently slumped. Computer leasing suffered a temporary setback, but revived strongly by the mid 1970s. In 1979, IBM introduced another new series of computers, the 434X series, and secondhand market values for many computers in the 370 series fell sharply. The resulting crisis in the computer leasing industry led to the collapse of Itel Corporation, the leading computer leasing company at the time.

Computer leasing revived again in the 1980s. Comdisco became the US market leader in financing secondhand computers. In the UK, one of the market leaders was Atlantic Computers.

UK computer leasing companies developed a fairly complex method of arranging lease finance. They would in many cases either

- arrange a lease with a customer and then assign the lease to a traditional equipment leasing company, or
- obtain funding for a lease from a traditional equipment leasing company by means of a head lease/sub-lease arrangement.

Sub-leasing equipment

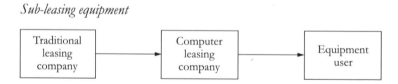

In these arrangements, the benefit of the capital allowances would be obtained by the head lessor, the traditional leasing company, not the computer leasing company. The computer leasing company relied heavily for its profits on the residual values of the leased equipment.

Atlantic Computers specialized in arranging leases with special flex options and walk options that, under regulations applying at that time, allowed lessees to classify them as operating leases and keep them off their balance sheet. Typically, a full payout lease would be written on a mainframe computer, for a seven-year term, but with break points for the lessee subject to giving periods of written notice. The break points were provided by

- a flex option after three years, giving the lessee the option to get rid of the existing computer and replace it with a more up-to-date IBM model on a new seven-year lease
- a walk option after five years, giving the lessee the option to walk away from the lease, to get rid of the computer without any commitment to take on a new lease for replacement equipment.

This type of seven-year lease was sometimes referred to as a 3/5/7, to signify the break points.

If the lessee exercised either of the options, Atlantic Computers would gain possession of the computer. It would then expect to terminate the original finance lease by making a termination payment to the head lessor out of the proceeds from selling the computer, that is out of the residual value.

In most cases, Atlantic supplied the lessee with asset finance by means of an arranged lease. Atlantic acted as a broker between the lessee and a lessor for a normal seven-year lease with a termination payment arrangement. Atlantic arranged the flex and walk options as a separate agreement with the lessee.

The advantage of this arrangement was to allow Atlantic Computers to discount the seven-year rental stream at a lower interest rate and take the full mark-up to profit in the first year without a reserve to cover future losses. While the assets on lease grew strongly, Atlantic Computers were able to generate sufficient cash to keep expanding the business, but it ran into problems as the recession began to bite in 1990.

Example
Equipment costing a notional $1,000 is sold on a 3/5/7 structure at a rental of $220 per annum. The present value of this rental stream over seven years at 10% is $1,178. The mark-up of $178 is taken as a gross margin in the first year leaving no reserve for possible losses in year five. In year five of this example, the settlement with two rentals of $220

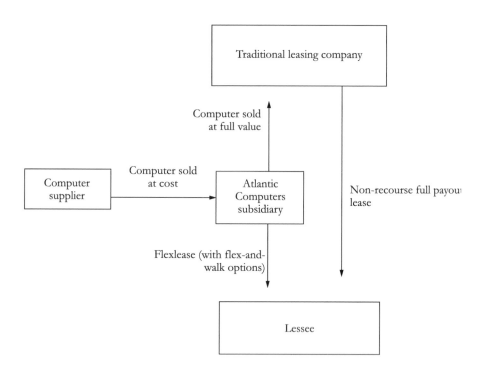

outstanding is $382 or over 39% of the original value. Computer equipment does not retain such a high value and therefore if a client walks at five years, it implies a considerable loss to the company providing the break option. The table of settlements discounted at 10% per annum is as follows:

Year	Date	Rental payments	Outstanding rents $	Settlement at 10% p.a	Example Value %	Equipment value	(Exposure) or cover $	Percent of settlement
0	Dec-98	220	1,320	958	40.0	400	(558)	(58.3)
1	Dec-99	220	1,320	958	40.0	400	(558)	(58.3)
2	Dec-00	220	1,100	834	30.0	300	(534)	(64.0)
3	Dec-01	220	880	697	20.0	200	(497)	(71.3)
4	Dec-02	220	660	547	10.0	100	(447)	(81.7)
5	Dec-03	220	440	382	5.0	50	(332)	(86.9)
6	Dec-04	220	220	200	0.0	0	(200)	(100.0)
Total		1,540						

The collapse of Atlantic in April 1990 occurred because of its accounting policies and the over-estimation of residual values. Actual residual values were insufficient to cover termination payments. Until the collapse, the problem was not apparent, and Atlantic reported a strong profit performance on the basis of assumed residual values.

In 1988, Atlantic Computers was acquired by British & Commonwealth Holdings plc (B&C) for £416 million. The financial collapse came just 19 months later. It was subsequently reported that Atlantic's walk liabilities, i.e. liabilities to make termination payments if a lessee exercised a walk option, exceeded the realizable value of the leased computers by over £100 million.

Customers of Atlantic lost their flexlease options with the company's collapse, leaving them unexpectedly with normal finance lease obligations to a traditional leasing company.

A lesson of the Atlantic Computers case history is the need for caution in estimating residual values on leased equipment and care in adopting prudent accounting policies that correctly match risk and reward.

Other Countries

Accounting for leases in many countries such as Australia, Canada, Germany and the Netherlands follows the same general rules as those in the US and the UK. However, the capitalization of finance lease assets is not mandatory in France, and finance lease assets are not capitalized at all in Japan and Italy.

An international accounting standard on accounting for leases (IAS17) was issued in 1982 and was revised in 1997. This, too, is based on the same principles as the US accounting standard (FAS 13) and the UK's SSAP 21. The standards continue to evolve as national accounting standards try to produce guidelines for distinguishing between operating leases and leases that provide economic ownership. With the introduction of the single currency in Europe and the move towards US Generally Accepted Accounting Practice (GAAP), further convergence is likely to occur over the next 10 to 20 years.

12

Leasing Developments

Leasing is well established in the US and the UK, and continues to develop in other countries, particularly in Europe. This chapter considers some of the more recent developments in the largest leasing market.

Small and Medium Ticket Leasing

In the US, the volume of leasing business has increased steadily over the past 10 years from $112.7 billion in 1988 to $183.4 billion forecast in 1998. But the penetration rate has stayed much the same over the past two years at 30.9%.

There has been some growth in small ticket leasing in recent years because it has been more difficult for small businesses to obtain bank loans. With bank credit hard to obtain, leasing has been one of the few ways many companies can finance new equipment. Leasing transactions valued at less than $25,000 accounted for more than one-quarter of all new leasing deals in the US in 1996.

The finance cost of small ticket leasing, however, has been very high. Leasing companies in the US have charged a much higher effective rate of interest than on bank loans to reflect the reduced security provided by leasing. This is a cost that small companies apparently have been willing to accept.

The main driving forces that are expected to impact the leasing market in 1999 as identified by the Industry Future Council at the ELA are relevant for the global leasing industry: the economy, the availability, cost and types of capital; technological change; developments in the market, such as availability of personnel; and changes in legislation and regulation.

The dramatic downturn in the capital markets from July to October 1998 meant it was much harder to get access to capital, both from a lessor's and lessee's point of view. This has also helped to encourage greater use of securitization. Nonetheless, it is still only worthwhile for large transactions, those over $100 million.

The speed of technological change has had, and will continue to offer, significant opportunities for lessors. The growth of internets and intranets, use of computer graphics and explosion in wireless communications are just some of the opportunities that have arisen. Software leasing too is a growing business.

In the UK, the recession in the 1990s appears to have resulted in a higher proportion of bad debts for leasing companies, particularly those leasing to small- and middle-sized customers. The problem of bad debts appears to have been much lower among medium ticket customers.

Big Ticket Leasing

The leasing market for big ticket items depends on the demand from large organizations for finance to support large capital expenditure projects. The UK big ticket leasing market has been given impetus in recent years from the continuing capital investment requirements of water, electricity supply and rail transportation companies. There appears to have been a recent trend in towards syndication of asset finance at lower ticket prices. In a syndicated arrangement, several leasing companies combine to provide the required finance.

Cross-Border Leasing

Cross-border leasing involves a lease agreement between a leasing company in one country and a lessee in another country. The cross-border leasing market originated in the US in the 1970s. US leasing companies were able to claim tax allowances on equipment under US tax regulations, and pass on the benefit in lower financing costs, to a lessee operating in a country where the same tax benefits did not apply.

Cross-border leasing (export leasing) continues to develop in Europe, but has not been widespread among UK leasing companies. This is because UK lessors can claim capital allowances against tax at only the very low rate of 10% per annum for assets leased abroad. This makes it difficult for UK leasing companies to compete against non-UK leasing companies outside the UK.

Other Developments

Several other trends have become evident in the industry. They include

- the growth of niche markets such as car leasing and vendor programs based on supplier relationships and partnerships
- the decline of extensive branch structures as bank-based finance companies have sought economies of scale
- consolidation of the industry as multinationals, such as Newcourt Credit of Canada and GE Capital, have increased their presence in Europe
- shifts to services/products to include maintenance, replacement equipment or other services
- an increase in true operating leases with more emphasis on managing portfolios of assets
- some refinement of the tax and accounting standards, for example IAS17
- increased use of securitization as a means of financing.

Conclusion

Despite recent developments, leasing has retained its basic advantages for lessees.

- It is an alternative to using cash resources or borrowing as a means of obtaining asset finance.
- Most leasing is asset-specific, and the lessee normally is not required to provide extra security. Leasing therefore provides an additional line of credit to the lessee that might not significantly affect its capacity to borrow from other sources.
- It can be a tax-efficient source of fixed rate medium-term finance, at a competitive rate of interest.
- The rental period and rental payments can be matched to the asset's anticipated life and expected revenue-earning characteristics.
- In the case of operating leases, it can satisfy the lessee's requirement to avoid reporting the assets and the asset finance on a balance sheets.

The lessor's only security in the event of default by the lessee is normally the asset itself and leasing companies should recognize that the value of the asset will be insufficient to protect the lessor against a bad debt. Leasing is in many cases, a partly secured term debt facility. The credit assessment of potential lessees now emphasizes ability to repay rather than the value of the asset as security.

Glossary

Add-On

A transaction to add related equipment to an existing lease. Typically, this term is used when the new equipment is financed using the same lease structure as was used in the underlying transaction except that the lease term for the add-on is set so that it expires co-terminously on the same date as the original transaction.

Advance Payments

Payments made by the lessee at the inception of a leasing transaction.

Amortization

A breakdown of periodic loan payments into two components: a principal portion and an interest portion.

APR

Annual Percentage Rate. The effective rate taking into account compounding and other fees.

Back-to-Back Leasing

Arrangement whereby a head lessor leases an asset to a sub-lessor, who then sub-leases the same asset to an end-user.

Balloon Rental

A substantially larger final rental payment at the end of the primary lease period.

Bargain-Purchase Option

An option given to the lessee to purchase the equipment on lease at a price that is less than the expected fair market value so that, at the inception of the lease, it is reasonable to assume that the lessee definitely will purchase the equipment on the option date.

Basis Point
A unit of measurement equal to 1/100th of a percent. For example, 25 basis points = .25%.

Big Ticket
Lease of an asset whose capital cost is very high, perhaps $20 million or even more.

Broker
Go-between who brings lessor and lessee together.

Capital Allowance
Allowance that can be claimed by the business owner of an asset, in a lease, the lessor, where a portion of the capital cost of the asset can be set off against taxable profits as a tax allowance.

Capital Lease (or finance lease)
Type of lease classified and accounted for by a lessee as a purchase and by the lessor as a sale or financing, if it meets any one of the following criteria; (a) the lessor transfers ownership to the lessee at the end of the lease term; (b) the lease contains an option to purchase the asset at a bargain price; (c) the lease term is equal to 75% or more of the estimated economic life of the property, there will be exceptions for used property leased toward the end of its useful life; or (d) the present value of the minimum lease rental payments is equal to 90% or more of the fair market value of the leased asset less related tax credits retained by the lessor. See finance lease.

Conditional sale lease
A lease that in substance is a conditional sale. Sometimes called a hire-purchase agreement, a money-over-money lease or a lease intended as security.

Co-terminous
Two or more leases that are linked so that both will terminate together.

Depreciation
A tax deduction representing a reasonable allowance for exhaustion, wear and tear and obsolescence, that is taken by the owner of the equipment

and by which the cost of the equipment is allocated over time. Depreciation decreases the company's balance sheet assets and is also recorded as an operating expense for each period. Various methods of depreciation are used that alter the number of periods over which the cost is allocated and the amount expensed each period.

Discount Rate

A certain interest rate that is used to bring a series of future cash flows to their present value. Use of a discount rate removes the time value of money from future cash flows.

Fair Market Value

The price for which property can be sold in an arms-length transaction, between informed, unrelated, and willing parties, each of which is acting rationally and in its own best interest.

Finance Lease (or Full-Payout Lease)

Lease for which the rentals in the primary period are sufficient for the lessor to recover substantially all of the capital cost of the asset and finance costs. See also Capital Lease.

Fixed-Purchase Option

An option given to the lessee to purchase the leased equipment from the lessor on the option date for a guaranteed price. Both the date and the price must be determined at the inception of the lease. A typical fixed purchase option is 10% of the original cost of the equipment.

Full-Payout Lease

A lease in which the total of the lease payments pays back to the lessor the entire cost of the equipment including financing, overhead and a reasonable rate of return, with little or no dependence on a residual value.

Hire Purchase (see also Conditional Sale Lease)

Agreement in which an asset is acquired by a user in return for periodic payments to a finance provider. At the end of an agreed term, the user obtains full ownership of the asset in return for a nominal payment.

Incremental Borrowing Rate

The rate that, at the inception of the lease, a lessee would have incurred to borrow over a similar term, funds necessary to purchase the leased asset.

Interest Variation
Clause in a lease agreement that provides for the rental to be altered, in line with movements in a benchmark rate of interest.

Lease
A contract through which an owner of equipment (the lessor) conveys the right to use its equipment to another party (the lessee) for a specified period of time (the lease term) for specified periodic payments.

Lease Purchase
Full payout, net leases structured with a term equal to the equipment's estimated useful life and a nominal lessee purchase on expiry.

Lease Schedule
A schedule to a master lease agreement describing the leased equipment, rentals and other terms applicable to the equipment.

Lessee
The party to a lease agreement who is obligated to pay the rentals to the lessor and is entitled to use and possess the leased equipment during the lease term.

Lessor
The party to a lease agreement who has legal or tax title to the equipment in the case of a true tax lease, grants the lessee the right to use the equipment for the lease term and is entitled to receive rental payments.

Leveraged Lease
Lease arrangement where the lessor obtains most of the finance to purchase the leased asset from a third party financier. The financier has recourse to the leased asset in the event of non-payment of rentals by the lessee, but has no recourse against the lessor.

Master Lease
A continuing lease arrangement whereby additional equipment can be added from time to time merely by describing that equipment in a new lease schedule executed by the parties. The original lease contract terms and conditions apply to all subsequent schedules. A master lease is, in

essence, a line of credit that can be drawn from over time in order to purchase equipment.

Middle Ticket
Lease of an asset with a middle range capital value, in the region of $200,000 to $17 million.

Novation
Replacement of the purchaser by a lessor as owner of an asset, in a situation where the prospective lessee has placed an order with the supplier to acquire the asset before the lease agreement is reached.

Off Balance Sheet Financing
A lease that qualifies as an operating lease for the lessee's financial accounting purposes. Such leases are referred to as off balance sheet financing because of their exclusion from the balance sheet asset and debt presentation, except for that portion of the payments due in the current fiscal period. Full disclosure of such transactions typically is made in the auditor's notes to the financial statements. Periodic payments are recorded as expense items on the lessee's income statement.

Operating Lease
A lease where the lessor does not recover the full cost of the asset through rentals received in the primary period. The lessor looks to the residual value of the asset at the end of the primary period for a substantial part of the capital recovery.

Payment in Advance
Periodic payments due at the beginning of each period.

Payment in Arrears
Periodic payments due at the end of each period.

Plant Hire
Short-term rental of plant, particularly to users in construction and related industries.

Present Value
The discounted value of a payment or stream of payments to be received in the future, taking into consideration a specific interest or discount rate.

Purchase Option
An option given to the lessee to purchase the equipment from the lessor, usually as of a specified date.

Real Estate Lease
Lease of land and buildings.

Rental Rebate
An amount paid by a lessor to the lessee at the end of a finance lease. Most usually paid when the lessee disposes of an asset on behalf of the lessor.

Residual Value
The book value that the lessor depreciates a piece of equipment down to during the lease term, typically based on an estimate of the future value, less a safety margin.

Sale and Leaseback
Arrangement whereby a leasing company purchases an asset from a client, and leases the same asset to the same client on normal leasing terms.

Sales-Aid Leasing (also Vendor Financing)
Leasing provided by an equipment supplier, either directly or by arrangement with a finance house to a customer, as a means of marketing the supplier's products. Leasing is used as an aid to selling.

Skip-Payment Lease
A lease that contains a payment stream requiring the lessee to make payments only during certain periods of the year.

Small Ticket Lease
Lease of a small-value asset valued around $10,000 to $500,000).

Step-Up or Step-Down
A feature of a lease that contain a payment stream that either increases (step-up) or decreases (step-down) in amount over the term of the lease.

Tax Variation
Clause in a lease agreement providing for a change in rental payments in the event of a change in the rate of corporation tax, or in tax regulations relating to leased assets.

Upgrade

To trade in leased equipment for a newer, more advanced model during the lease term.

Useful Life

The period of time during which an asset will have economic value and be usable. The useful life of an asset is sometimes called the economic life of the asset. To qualify as an operating lease, the property must have a remaining useful life of 25% of the original estimated useful life of the leased property at the end of the lease term, and at least a life of one year.

Vendor Financing

Leasing provided by an equipment supplier, either directly or by arrangement with a finance house, to a customer as a means of marketing the supplier's products. Leasing is used as an aid to selling.

Index